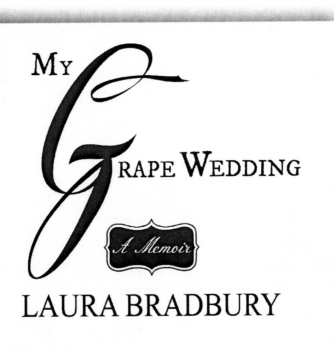

My Grape Wedding

A Memoir

LAURA BRADBURY

Published by Grape Books

www.laurabradbury.com

Copyright © 2016 Laura Bradbury

ISBN 13: 978-0-9921583-8-5

"Le mariage est une vie dans la vie."

-Honoré de Balzac

"Mariage pluvieux, mariage heureux."

-Proverbe Français

.

This one, *bien sûr*, is for my husband but also for his Mémé Germaine who never failed to be the life and soul of every *fête*.

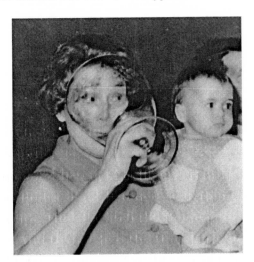

CHAPTER 1

Kathmandu, Nepal

The rickshaw lurched to a stop, throwing Franck and me against the glass partition decorated with posters of Bollywood stars and Hindu deities.

"*Ça va?*" Franck pulled me back and ran a hand over my dusty face, as if to make sure I was more or less intact.

"What was it?" I asked. "Another cow?"

Cows and yaks were kings of the road in Kathmandu. Drivers would much rather cause a major traffic pileup involving several human fatalities than harm a hair of a sacred bovine. These animals wandered through the main streets with impunity, usually with their eyes traced in thick kohl and their necks adorned with necklaces made from threaded orange geraniums.

I peeked out the rickshaw and saw a crowd of gesticulating Nepalis, and about thirty screeching monkeys hopping all over the tangle of rickshaws and cars in the road.

I leaned back. "Monkeys. If it's not cows, it's monkeys."

It was amazing how, in a matter of weeks, Franck and I had adapted to the chaos of life in Kathmandu, our new home base for the next three months as we volunteered with Operation Eyesight in surgical eye camps in rural Nepal.

Our first camp had been a thirteen-hour bus ride from Kathmandu on the Nepal-Indian border, in a village so isolated most of the villagers had never seen a Caucasian before. We were given a welcome dinner served on lily pads on the porch of the chief's mud hut, and the entire village came to watch us eat. It was breathtaking and disorienting all at once. That village's remoteness had made Kathmandu seem like the epitome of civilization.

I peered at the scribbled address written on a scrap of paper I held in my hand. "The place must be near here."

Franck paid the rickshaw driver—we noticed that the rates the drivers charged us fell at the same speed that our Nepali improved. We weren't paying as little as locals quite yet, but we were paying significantly less than before.

I made my way to the side of the unpaved road, dodging another rickshaw and a cart filled with some type of large green fruit.

Franck joined me. "So, we're close?"

I tried to make out a number—any number—posted on the row of shopfronts in front of us. "Hard to say. It's great to have a street address, but what would make the system work even *better* would be shopkeepers actually putting street addresses on their stores."

"That would make it quicker," Franck mused, "but far less interesting." He took the paper and ducked into the dark doorway closest to us.

"*Namaste!*" Franck bowed his head and pressed his two hands together, a gesture that over the past month had become as natural to us as breathing. The man behind the counter seemed, as far as I could tell, to be selling gold- and jewelry-encrusted horns from enormous yaks. Intriguing, but not what we were looking for. He took the scrap of paper from Franck and read the address.

I was glad for us to have this little project of searching for one of the most under-the-radar jewelry shops in Kathmandu. A hidden treasure, according to the Irish nurse who worked with us.

On coming back to Kathmandu after the camp, we'd found a number of faxes waiting for us—for me, more accurately—with news from my father that he had sent off all the law school applications that I had prepared before leaving Canada.

Franck had shaken his head with obvious frustration when he read the faxes. "Law school in England? I just don't get it Laura. Why don't we try to work together on the photojournalism thing?"

2

"We'll never earn enough money to live doing that," I said, thinking about the small checks we had received for the few articles we'd published in magazines over the past couple of years. "One of us has to be pragmatic."

"And where do I fit in? What am I supposed to do in England while you're busy being pragmatic?"

"Can't you just support my plans?" I said, frustrated. "It's not as if you have a better one that will actually pay for food and a roof over our heads."

"You don't have to go to law school." Franck had tried to convince me. "I know we'll figure something else out. Have faith that we can."

But I wasn't brought up to have faith. Unlike Franck, I knew that life didn't just take care of itself—that was a pipe dream. I had to take care of myself, take care of both of us actually, because I was the designated planner of us, the couple. How could Franck not see that one of us, at least, had to plan and strategize? How could he resent me for that when I was only trying to do what was necessary?

Looking for the jewelry shop was a much-needed distraction from that unresolved conflict that kept bubbling up between us.

The man inside the yak horn shop nodded and gave Franck directions in a fast flow of Nepali, which he embellished with eloquent hand gestures and head tilts, and which I couldn't follow at all.

As we walked out of the shop after thanking him, I whispered to Franck, "Did you catch any of that?"

"Three doors down," he said. "Or maybe thirty. Not entirely sure."

In the end, I was the one who spotted it. Actually, what caught my eye was an exceedingly chic-looking woman sitting in front of a shop counter, appearing entirely out of place. Several gemstones casually scattered on the counter flashed in the dusty afternoon light.

I pulled Franck inside. "This looks promising."

"*Namaste.*" We greeted the two men standing behind the counter, both of whom wore yellowish-white Daura Suruwal—loose pants with a long tunic overtop, which most Nepali men wore.

I tried to explain in my broken Nepali that I was interested in getting a necklace made for my birthday, as a special keepsake from our trip. Franck, in the meantime, sat down on the other available stool and chatted with the chic woman who, *quelle surprise*, turned out to be from Paris.

3

My eyes opened wide at the sparkling gems splayed out in front of her. Rubies, diamonds, even some emeralds. Franck and I didn't have much money at all. I felt worried—what if this store *looked* like an unassuming hole-in-the-wall, but made only expensive jewelry?

"I've just been in Tahiti," she said to Franck in a nasal Parisian accent. "I bought the most *sublime* black pearls, so I decided to stop by Kathmandu on the way home to Paris to get them set here. They always know what to do. I thought I'd make up a few other little treats for myself as well. I have the idea for the most glorious ring!"

She began inspecting the gems with the tip of her long, manicured fingernail while the other man behind the counter gestured at us to sit further down.

"What can I help you with?" he asked in heavily accented but excellent English.

"I'm interested in having a necklace made," I said. "Or maybe a ring...I'm not entirely sure."

"A ring?" Franck asked, an odd look on his face. "You hadn't mentioned a ring."

"I thought of it just now. I don't wear necklaces all the time, but I do wear rings every day." I held up my hands to show my silver ring with a cool, opaque purple stone in the middle of some silver squiggles. It wasn't valuable, but I had always liked it. On my other hand, I wore a round blue flash moonstone set in intricate silver.

Franck peered at my fingers. "You know what would look nice? An engagement ring."

"What are you talking about?" I laughed. "I wouldn't get an engagement ring unless we were going to get mar—"

Franck's eyes widened. He looked as surprised by his suggestion and its implications as I was.

"Are you suggesting what I think you're suggesting?" I asked.

"I think so...*oui.*"

I couldn't speak right away. I'd never expected this—especially then, when we had such a fundamental disagreement about the future direction of our lives hovering between us. "Have you been thinking about it for long?" I wondered out loud.

"*Non,*" Franck said, "the idea just occurred to me right now. I know we have always said we don't need a marriage certificate to make what we have between us real, but still...what do you think?"

A wedding? Getting married? We had always disdained the concept of taking the traditional route. Still, I realized that I already felt married to Franck in many ways.

"It would be an opportunity for a great party," Franck said.

"Maybe two great parties," I said. "One in Burgundy, one in Victoria."

Franck's eyes lit up, the idea of marrying me or two massive family celebrations—I couldn't be sure which—obviously thrilling him.

The Nepali man was waiting for us, watching this exchange with avid eyes. "This is not how it happens in Nepal," he said.

"How does it happen in Nepal?" Franck asked.

"The families of the young woman and the young man make the match. It is not something that is decided by the couple themselves. Often, they only meet once or twice before the wedding ceremony, sometimes not at all. That is how it was for me and my wife. We are happy. So happy. We have two sons." Pride glowed in his wide smile. From what I had seen so far, sons were the ultimate treasure in Nepali society. "It is the best way," he said. "The Nepali way."

"If we waited for our parents to set us up, we never would have met," I said. "We're from different countries."

"Oh…that does makes it more complicated," the man admitted.

"We had to fight to be together."

"Fight?" the man said. "Did you win?"

I looked over at Franck. *Engagement rings. A wedding. Probably wedding rings as well…* "Did we just get engaged?" I asked him.

Franck's hazel eyes sparkled. "I think so."

Franck and I exchanged shell-shocked looks.

The man clapped his hands together and bowed his head. "I wish you great happiness," he said. "And many, many sons."

CHAPTER 2

During the week that our engagement (how strange that the word applied to us now) rings were being made up in Kathmandu, we travelled fifteen hours to a surgical eye camp in another remote village on the India-Nepal border. Nobody seemed entirely sure, in fact, whether the camp was technically located in Nepal or had, in fact, strayed over the border into India.

Just hours before we left the Lions Eye Care Center with the medical team and all the equipment to go to the central bus station in Kathmandu, I was handed a fax by the head doctor, Dr. Pradhan, a charming man from Sikkim, an isolated part of Northern India. "This just arrived for you from Canada."

Fax machines were few and far between in the city, and we were lucky that we had access to one at the eye care center.

"You must be careful with that box!" He turned and began to direct his assistant, Shyam, in the correct packing of the surgical instruments they would be using.

"What does it say?" Franck asked, who was going through his camera case and counting his rolls of film. One of our duties was to document the camp activities and take photos for fundraising efforts that we could use after our return to Canada.

I read over the fax once. Then again. And then a third time to make sure I wasn't making a mistake. I wasn't quite sure how I was going to break the news to Franck. It should be good news, and it *was* but... "My dad just received a letter. From England."

Franck looked up. "And?"

"I've been accepted to Oxford to study law."

Franck remained silent for a few beats, then smiled a forced smile that I knew from experience wasn't a real smile so much as a grimace. "*Félicitations*," he said. "I didn't even know you applied to Oxford."

It had been an afterthought, actually. The way the application process in the UK was set up, I could apply to five law programs with the same application, then choose between applying to Oxford or Cambridge. Nobody was allowed to apply to both. I had simply applied to Oxford because I was doing all the other applications anyway.

"I never thought I'd get in," I said. "Not in a million years."

Franck occupied himself with taking off a wide-angle lens and screwing on a longer one. "So," he said finally, "are you thinking about accepting their offer?"

The question highlighted the vast chasm between our upbringings. To me, going to Oxford was the pinnacle of everything that I'd been groomed to want in life when I attended my exclusive private school. Prestige. Achievement. Status. Money. It would be unthinkable to refuse *Oxford*. Franck—I could tell from his tone of voice—honestly didn't see it the same way, nor was he certain I would accept. Oxford, for him, barely registered as different from the other British universities I had applied to, such as Bristol. That unspoken hierarchy of achievement was not part of his lexicon.

"I can't turn down Oxford," I explained.

He nodded tersely.

"Maybe we can still do some articles on the side," I said. "I'm sure I'll have some spare time. I've heard tutorials at Oxford only take up a few hours a week, and the rest of your time is your own. There are hardly any lectures."

Franck shrugged. "Yup. We'll see."

"Do you still want to get married?" I came out and asked the foremost question in my mind.

He looked up, his eyes wide. "Of course. Don't you?"

"Yes. *Bien sûr*," I said. "This doesn't change anything. Oxford will be a great place for us, and the program is only two years because I already have an undergraduate degree."

He nodded. "I'm happy for you Laura. I am. Just give me a little while to get used to the idea."

Seven hours into the seemingly endless bus ride, Franck was still quieter than usual. He hadn't lost his gallantry and had given me the seat beside the window, while he sat on the aisle beside two goats and a chicken, also passengers on the bus. We had spent enough time in Nepal not to question this. The driver had put a Bollywood movie into the VCR, which was incorporated into an ancient TV set that hung perilously in the upper corner of the bus, just behind the driver's seat. The music was blasting, and women wearing colorful saris performing a dance number involving an improbable number of gushing marble water fountains filled the screen.

All of the passengers on the bus, with the exception of Franck, me, and the livestock, were singing along to the film. Behind us sat Shyam and a lovely new ophthalmic assistant who looked similar to his age. This was her first camp, I knew. They were singing the duet together, and I noticed their voices were more beautiful than the tinny sound of the actors' voices on the screen.

"You're quiet," I said to Franck.

He looked over at me. "I'm thinking."

I waited a few minutes, hoping he would elaborate—but no such luck.

"About Oxford?" I prompted.

"Yes."

I stuffed down impatience. Even if I wasn't happy about something, I was brought up to *pretend* that I was at least. That was another difference between us. Franck's family never feigned any emotion for the sake of manners. When they were angry, they yelled, sulked, sulked for hours and sometimes days, and occasionally threw things. When they were sad, they wept. When they were happy, they laughed and danced.

Getting into Oxford was a huge achievement. Couldn't Franck just act happy for me without making it so complicated?

The goat in the aisle beside me rested his head in my lap and began to nibble on the seam of my denim shirt.

But it *was* complicated. We were getting married. What affected one of us would affect the other. That was more or less how we had been living since we met anyway, but something about making it official made it so much more...concrete.

The bus screeched to a stop, and I peered out my window to see shacks and kerosene lights punching holes in the pitch dark of the roadside. My stomach gurgled. Dinner stop, undoubtedly the ubiquitous yet (usually) extremely palatable *dahl bhaht*—curried lentils over rice.

"Don't worry." Franck turned to me as I waited for the goats and the chicken to clear the aisle so we could get up. "I'll get used to it. It's just I don't process things as fast as you do. I need time."

Time. I needed to dig deep to find some patience, something that was chronically in short supply *chez moi.*

"I understand," I said. "We can talk about it when you're ready. Come on. Let's go get our *dahl.*"

Orange light tinted the desert landscape. The jeep that had driven us three hours from the bus station in Siliguri now rolled into a small village consisting of mud huts adorned with beautiful, painted symbols on their exterior walls. In the center of the village was one concrete building that Dr. Pradhan told me housed the local school and administration offices. This is where we would be setting up the surgical eye camp. The building was low enough that I could see the desert, punctuated with only the odd stunted tree or bush, stretched out beyond it.

A trio of village woman in dusty orange, fuchsia, and saffron saris walked with riveting grace toward the fiery ball of the rising sun, balancing metal bowls on their heads.

We were a world away from anything either Franck or I had ever known, just like we had been in the first camp. Still, just as I had the last time, with Franck nearby, I didn't feel nearly as lost in this foreign landscape as I had expected to. He was like a little portable home for me, no matter where we were. I hoped I would always be the same for him, there in deepest rural Nepal, or Canada, or Oxford.

I turned back to the building behind me to see that, during my few minutes of gazing at the landscape, a line of at least fifty people had formed in front of a card table that Shyam was unfolding in front of the building. One of my jobs at the previous camp was to record the name, age, and village of each patient on their arrival before passing them off to the doctor for a preliminary exam.

Shyam waved me over and tilted his head in the way that was the precursor for most conversations in Nepal. "*Thik cha?*" he asked. How are you?

I found myself mirroring his gesture. "*Thik cha,*" I answered. Good. But in fact, Franck still hadn't talked further about Oxford, and I had just had an almost sleepless night, between the goat that was determined to make a meal out of my clothes and worries about Oxford and Franck spinning around and around in my mind to the soundtrack of Bollywood movies.

"There are far more people than we anticipated," Shyam said. "Would you mind starting now? I will make sure somebody brings you some chai."

"Sure," I said.

Even though Shyam was from one of the lower castes and had to fight to be properly educated, his English was excellent. He had always been a good student, he confessed to me shortly after we first met, and had perfected his English when he was studying to be a medical assistant in the Indian city of Bangalore. It was there, he told me, that he had begun to dream of one day opening an optical store of his own.

I sat down on a rickety stool behind the card table and was instantly swarmed by the crowd of people.

Shyam shouted in Nepali for everyone to line up properly. This ignited many dramatic scenes fit for the Bollywood films on the bus, with people in line pleading and crying. Shyam proved to be made of solid stuff, though, because he shouted something I didn't understand,

and everyone fell back into something that resembled a queue.

Shyam slid the patient registration book in front of me and handed me three sharpened pencils.

"*Dhanyabahd*, Shyam," I said. "Thank you" was one of the phrases we had taught ourselves with the help of our pocket guide to Nepali on the flight from Bangladesh to Kathmandu.

I looked up to see an elderly woman wearing a faded pink sari modestly draped over her head. Her eyes were almost completely opaque with cataracts.

"*Namaste*," I said, and nodded to her in case she wasn't completely blind, which I doubted.

"*Tapaiko nahm ke ho?*" I asked. I had been taught this phrase, which means "what is your name" in the first five minutes of our first camp.

"Srita Devi," the woman answered, and burst into tears.

Two hours of registrations went by, with me sustained by three glasses of warm chai tea, always welcome with its cardamom-infused sweetness. I was finishing the last few drops of my third glass when a young man who was next in line stepped up to my desk. Behind him, he dragged a young boy of about four or five years, who was determined to hide behind his legs. I squinted up at the man's eyes but couldn't make out any discernible cataracts. However, they held a desperation that made me straighten my slouch and pay attention. The boy, I noticed, was pressing a hand against his right ear. They had to be father and son.

"*Namaste*." I greeted them, and then the man began to talk to me in a fast river of Nepali that I couldn't understand, while trying to pull his son out from behind his legs and clucking at him to remove his hand from his ear.

When he finally managed to show me his son's ear, I gasped. The ear was bright red and inflamed to almost two times its normal size.

Looking deep inside it, I could make out the end of a metal coil, like a small spring that had come loose from a piece of machinery. I came to understand from the father's gestures that his son had stuck it in his ear, something I might have done at his age. As a child I was forever swallowing chess pieces or shoving plastic beads up my nostrils. I don't know why some children have to explore the world in such a direct way. But this wasn't the first little boy to stick a foreign object in his ear, nor would he be the last.

I gestured at them to wait just a moment. "Shyam!" I called over to him. He had set up his station on a card table like mine a few meters away and was busy performing preliminary eye exams on the cataract patients. "I need your help."

Shyam came over quickly, and I outlined the little boy's dilemma. As gently as possible, Shyam made a cursory inspection of the boy's ear. "That doesn't look good," he said to me in English under his breath. "I must find Dr. Pradhan."

Dr. Pradhan was the most respected and experienced doctor in the camp. His kind manner and devotion to curing blindness in the most remote regions of Nepal made him a saint-like figure at the eye hospital in Kathmandu. Shyam ushered him over, and I stood to give him my seat. He performed a thorough exam of the boy's ear right then and there. He tried to be gentle, but the boy's ear was so inflamed and infected that he began to cry, and then to wail. He must have been terrified and in absolute agony.

I wanted to reach out and take his hand and tell him that the doctors would make him all better—that he had come to the right place. Even though the doctors there were specialized in eyes, surely removing a foreign object from an eardrum wasn't beyond their capacities, I thought. *They must have antibiotics to clear up infections.*

Dr. Pradhan finally finished his exam, placed his narrow hand with his skilled, tapered fingers on the boy's head as if he were giving him a blessing, and said a few words. Then he stood and put his arm around the father, steering him away from his son and the line, and talking to him in a low voice. After a few steps, the man crumpled to the ground and began to weep. Several people, who must have been family members, rushed in and lifted him up and carried him away, scooping his son away from the crowd of people as well. I could hear the father's sobs as he was pulled away reverberating in my torso.

Dr. Pradhan came over and exchanged a few words with Shyam before going back inside the school building to oversee the splashing of Dettol on the floor, which constituted creating a sterile surgical environment for the operations the next day.

"What happened?" I demanded of Shyam. I was angry and confused. *Surely...*

"There was nothing we could do for the boy," Shyam said, looking down at the card table.

"But that's not possible. Dr. Pradhan could extract the spring and treat him with antibiotics, no?"

"It was too far in," Shyam said. "Not to mention too inflamed and infected. We don't have the proper surgical tools or adequate antibiotics. His infection is well beyond oral antibiotics now, and we have no IV equipment. Attempting to save him wouldn't work, and would only lead to far more suffering."

"But what is going to happen to him?" I asked, my mind not wanting to accept the bleak reality that was becoming obvious.

"Septicemia, which Dr. Pradhan feels has already set in. The best he and his family can hope for is a quick death. If Dr. Pradhan could possibly have saved him, he would have tried. Trust me."

My North American mind just couldn't seem to compute Shyam's sad but resigned attitude toward the tragic situation. The boy was so young. He should have had his whole life in front of him. If he was in any developed country, or even Kathmandu, he most likely could have been saved.

Shyam must have read the distress in my eyes. "Death is part of life, Laura," he said. "Don't you believe in reincarnation?"

"No," I said. "Well, I don't know. I've never really thought much about it," I answered vaguely as I searched the crowd for the boy and his father. They seemed to have vanished into thin air.

"In Nepal we believe in reincarnation. Perhaps the boy is meant to die, and there is hope he will be reborn into a higher caste, or a better life."

I blinked back tears. I was both moved and horrified by Shyam's attitude of surrender. And as for the boy—how I wanted to help that boy.

"The line is still long." Shyam used his chin to indicate the line of people at my desk, which snaked around the outbuilding. "Perhaps we cannot help that boy, but we should not allow that to stop us from helping others."

I went back to my registrations, my mind still spinning. Between new arrivals I looked desperately for Franck. I needed to tell him about the boy. The injustice bubbled up in my chest until it felt like it was going to explode.

Finally, I caught sight of Franck making his way over to my table with another glass of hot chai for me, two cameras slung around his neck and his bag of lenses dangling down his back.

I motioned for the elderly man who was next in line to wait just a moment. "I need to talk to you," I said.

Franck peered at the line, which just kept growing instead of getting smaller. "What's wrong?" he asked.

"There was a man who brought a little boy here. He was…I don't know…maybe four years old. He had stuck a metal spring in his ear." I quickly told Franck what had happened. "He's going to die, Franck. We can't just sit here and do nothing."

Franck studied me. "What can we do?"

"I don't know. There has to be something."

Franck paused a moment more, deep in thought. "Haven't you noticed that Nepalis accept death as a part of life in a way we don't in either France or Canada? It's different, but maybe it is not all bad."

I thought about the father collapsing onto the red dirt. "It *is* for that little boy! And his family!" I ended on a sob.

"We can't control everything, Laura," Franck said. "If Dr. Pradhan couldn't help him, how can we?"

I was struck by my powerlessness. All my resources—doctors, friends, access to medicines and surgeons—all of that was half a planet away in Canada. "It's not good enough," I said.

"It has to be."

The people in the line had begun to complain, so I had no choice but to start up again with my registrations, my heart hurting and my chest weighed down with anguish.

WHOLESALERS REMAINDERS COM LLC
742 ANDERSON ROAD NORTH
ROCK; HILL, SC; 29730

W 0.62 Standard   S10.02 P0.22

Shipped to:

Joseph Ford
PO BOX 361
CARMEL BY THE SEA, CA 93921-0361

ISBN / Title

0992158389 Qty - 1

My Grape Wedding (The Grape Series #2)

If you have received defective or incorrectly shipped merchandise, please notify Customer Service at (803)327-9028 within 7 days and follow their instructions for returns. Original shipment and handling charges are not refundable, and you will be responsible for all costs associated with return shipment. No COD returns will be accepted - Return postage is not included in Media rate shipping.
So you CAN NOT just mark the package Return to sender! If the item is received after the 90 day limit on returns has passed, no refund will be issued on the transaction.

If you need an itemized Receipt you will need to obtain it from your Amazon.com account.

Return Label

From:

Joseph Ford
PO BOX 361
CARMEL BY THE SEA, CA 93921-0361

To: 102-5227881-3626645

Returns/BooKnack
742 ANDERSON ROAD NORTH
Rock Hill, SC 29730

CHAPTER 3

I eventually had to stop the registrations, not because there were no more people in line but because dusk had fallen and there was no electricity.

I had a pounding headache—a toxic result, I was sure, of my seething anger, grief, and fear that had nowhere to go.

Shyam came over and took the registration book out from under me. "*Dhanyabahd*, Laura," he said. "Please come and join us for dinner before going to bed." He indicated a little bonfire, which I could see flickering in the distance.

I went over to it and sat down in a cross-legged position in the dirt. That was how most meals were eaten in the camps, and I was now used to it. I was so exhausted that I was tempted to curl up in the dust. On the fire, there was a two-tiered, aluminum cooking pot for the *dahl bhaht*. Two men of lower castes were busy stirring it and adding wood to the fire to make sure the temperature remained constant.

Franck sat down behind me, and I collapsed into his chest. As for all of our misunderstandings—those could wait until tomorrow.

I wondered where the little boy and his father were now. Had they begun to head back to their village, wherever that was? Had they just chosen a spot in the desert for the father to help his son die? My heart pounded with the possibilities.

Talk was desultory. Everyone had been working countless hours without a break and was in a hurry to get some food into their bodies and then get to sleep.

"You are still sad about that boy," Dr. Pradhan said.

"Yes," I said, feeling yet another burst of anger detonate in my chest. "He was so young and otherwise healthy. It's just a silly thing that children do, to stick something they shouldn't in their ear. I just can't accept that he has to die for a silly mistake."

Dr. Pradhan nodded. "It is sorrowful, but we must learn to let go. What is a life? It is not so much, really. Mine isn't. Neither is yours. You Westerners—" he shook his head "—you grip everything so hard. So many things are out of our control, but that does not mean that we do not try to help where we can. I said a prayer for him and his family."

Those words sounded familiar—Franck had said basically the same thing earlier in the day. Still, none of that calmed the storm raging underneath my breastbone. "I just can't reconcile it," I said. "It makes no sense."

"All I know," said Dr. Pradhan, his eyes taking on an otherworldly sheen in the dancing light of the flames, "is that life is joy, and life is tragedy, and life is mostly everything messy in between. We must celebrate the joy and accept the tragedy, and most of all do what we can to help during the messy, confusing parts."

One of the cooks handed me an aluminum plate divided into sections, each piled high with rice, curried lentils, and two different types of vegetables.

"*Dhanyabahd.*" I bowed my head.

"Besides," Dr. Pradhan added, "who ever said that life was supposed to make sense to us mere humans? I don't believe we will understand until after we have shed our human bodies."

That wasn't how I knew life. There was fatalism in Dr. Pradhan's attitude, and in the attitude of most of the Nepalis I had met in fact, which was anathema to my approach to life.

Yes, there was happiness, and even joy, but my life was also a race to diminish unpleasantness, to control outcomes and futures the way I would with my law degree. I suspected that Franck could relate more to Dr. Pradhan and Shyam's view of the world than I did.

I ate in silence and went to bed tortured by a sense of things not being resolved to my satisfaction.

Franck and I lay under the mosquito net. We had zipped our sleeping bags together and laid them down on the piece of plywood that served as a bed.

As hot as it was during the day, the desert temperature always plummeted at night. The generators we had brought with us for electricity would never be wasted on something as superfluous as heat.

Our team slept in the school building, which was the only concrete structure in the village—everything else was built of mud and straw. There were walls between the room where Franck and I slept and the two single rooms beside us where Shyam and Sita, the new ophthalmic assistant, slept.

Sita was a beautiful girl with natural grace, thick, shiny black hair, and eyes that were an unusual color of gray-green. As we finished off our last chai of the day, Shyam had confided to me that her eyes were the physical stamp of her high caste. He had said this in a voice tinged with regret. He had a crush on her; that much was obvious. I suspected it was mutual—she seemed to be with him all the time and laughed and smiled a lot in his presence. Shyam was the kind of person who made you smile, yet he could never be an acceptable husband for Sita due to his lowly caste.

There were no doors on the rooms, and the walls between them stopped about a foot from the ceiling, meaning that we could hear rustles and bumps as Shyam and Sita got themselves ready for bed.

My thoughts went again to the little boy. Had he died yet? I hoped his pain wasn't too bad. I couldn't even imagine the anguish of the father and the mother, wherever she was if she was alive. I could tell by his breathing that Franck hadn't fallen asleep yet either.

Silence, with the exception of some yaks lowing in the distance, eventually descended over the building.

I couldn't understand the world we'd been thrust into. Why wasn't life just happiness all the time? Why was suffering woven so tightly into the human experience—didn't it render the whole enterprise of living futile from its inception?

Just then, Shyam's voice floated over the partial wall between our rooms. He was singing the male part in the Bollywood love song that he and Sita had been singing on the bus.

Sita's voice, a crystal clear soprano, joined his a few seconds later as she sang the female parts. I couldn't understand the Hindi words, but I could tell that the song was about a couple who loved each other and were being kept apart by external forces—perhaps family or a vendetta or, as was truly the case, by the Hindu caste system.

I let their beautiful voices filled with sadness and longing wash over me. I had been right—their voices were even better than the soundtrack of the movie. I imagined Sita lying in her bed on one side of the wall and Shyam lying in his bed on his side of the wall, singing their hearts out, with each other saying all the things that they were not allowed to say in their own words.

Tears rolled down my face, pooling in my ears. I was in awe that such beauty could exist in the midst of this confusing, soul-destroying life. How could love—that thing that we could neither see nor touch—be resilient enough to keep sprouting up in the midst of all of our struggles?

Franck's hand moved toward me under our sleeping bags and covered mine. We wove our fingers together. As we lay there side by side, I reveled in the privilege of hearing Shyam and Sita sing, until their voices quieted and their song was just a transcendent memory.

CHAPTER 4

Oxford, United Kingdom, Hilary Term
February (Nine months after returning from Nepal)

My thigh muscles burned as I pedaled my bike through Little
Clarendon Street on my way home from my tutorial at Keble College.
The wicker basket attached to the front of my bike was loaded down
with casebooks, as was my backpack. Biking, our transportation in
Oxford, was uncomfortable because of my engagement ring from
Kathmandu—a large, rectangular-cut yellow topaz in a silver setting
that I designed myself. It always swung around on my finger when I
squeezed my brakes.

It was mid-February, a month into Hilary term, the second of three
terms of the academic year at Oxford. In the archaic ways of my new
school, it was named "Hilary" term because it followed the feast of
Saint Hilary of Poitiers on January fourteenth. I was growing
accustomed to the fact that Oxford existed in its own reality, which
was more often than not completely divorced from the reality of the
rest of the world.

I couldn't believe we were actually going to hold not one but two
wedding parties in six months' time. And not only two wedding parties
but two wedding parties separated geographically by a continent and
the Atlantic Ocean.

My parents were thrilled with the news that Franck and I were engaged. They adored Franck, and my mother informed me that it had come as a pleasant surprise that I would do anything as conventional as get married before having children. That made me laugh, as studying law at Oxford was hardly the behavior of a rebel.

The problem was that I had no to time to be a bride-to-be. Lounging around with wedding magazines was inherently incompatible with being a student of jurisprudence, otherwise known to most of the western world as law, and at Oxford, reputed to be one of the toughest degrees. Our lives couldn't have been more different from how they had been when we got engaged in Nepal. I often thought about Shyam and the little boy at the camp, and still wrestled with how I was to make sense of the jumble of good and bad I had witnessed over there, and in subsequent camps as well. Oxford was a town of privilege and achievement, yet in some way I felt more out of place there than I had in Nepal.

I slowed down beside the newsstand. A new issue of *Hello!* magazine was out, with a dashing photo of fourteen-year-old Prince William on the cover. I needed to head back to our flat and start in on the reading for my next essay, due in two days, but I was desperate for a break.

Not only did I find a law degree at Oxford extremely difficult but, to complicate matters, I'd also been placed in an accelerated program, which meant I had to complete the degree in two years instead of the usual three.

My thoughts flitted to my years studying English and French Literature at McGill University in Montreal. Instead of trying to analyze case after case of lawsuits, my homework then had consisted of reading *Great Expectations* or delving into the folklore of Irish fairy tales. I'd loved it.

By the end of my first week at Oxford, I knew that, in stark contrast to my literature degree, I hated studying law. I hated reading about people doing terrible things and bickering with one another. I hated the bone-dry nature of the cases we had to read and analyze. It was all very detail oriented, nitpicky, and so mind-numbingly boring. Every day I had to send a bucket deep, deep down into my well of willpower just to keep doing the work. For some reason, I had always thought I would find studying law fascinating, not because it *had* ever really fascinated me but because I had always felt that it *should* fascinate me. I mean, what was I supposed to do with a literature degree? I tried to make myself care, but I just didn't—which was a huge problem because I found the volume of work itself crushing. I had to work straight through the night at least twice every week just to get my assigned reading and tutorial essays done.

It was a far cry from the image I had painted of Oxford for Franck—lots of free time to visit castles and lounge in pubs—when we were at the eye hospital in Kathmandu.

"Are you just going to stare, or are you going to buy something?" the stand owner demanded. Since moving to Oxford, I'd discovered, much to my shock, that the British were not always polite. I had two theories: One, there were just way too many people per square kilometer in Southern England, compared to Canada where each citizen probably had three square kilometers to themselves. And two, the people of Oxford were fed up with the entitled attitude of students who swanned in and out of their city as though it was *their* own personal playground. I couldn't really blame them for either.

"Wake up, Miss!" he snapped when I didn't answer right away. I clutched one of the wings of my black academic gown that I had to wear to all tutorials. Maybe I didn't do so well with so little sleep after all...I'd been drifting off into dreamland all that day.

I grabbed a copy of *Hello!* and passed three pounds to the man, who grunted something unintelligible.

I smiled at him, as we did in Canada, but he just looked at me as if I were insane. The English were rather like the French in that respect— my Canadian habit of plastering a smile on my face all the time, no matter what I was actually feeling, just made them think I was deranged, or simple.

Before coming to Oxford, I had assumed that, because all my ancestors either hailed from Scotland, Ireland, or England, I would be considered an honorary Brit myself. This was not the case. On the contrary, the British assumed I was American, and when I dared point out that I was, in fact, Canadian they informed me there was no difference between the two.

I biked past the old church that housed the Freud café and onto Great Clarendon Street, where Franck and I were now settled in our modest two-bedroom flat. I bargained with myself as I pushed the pedals. I would give myself twenty minutes to read *Hello!* and then I would start right in on my reading for my next essay.

I knew Franck wasn't home yet. He was traveling back to Oxford from Paris on the Eurostar and was probably somewhere in the vicinity of Lille at that very moment. He'd been in Paris shooting society photos for Moët & Chandon at some big Dom Pérignon-sponsored *soirée* at Versailles. He'd landed the gig through a friend of ours who was an *attachée de presse* at the Champagne house.

Every two weeks or so, Franck would whip over to Paris via the Eurostar, snap a few photos at some gilded high society event—which inevitably involved the ubiquitous Gérard Depardieu—then come back to Oxford. I'd even begun to spot a few of his photos in *Paris Match* magazines.

It was pretty much a dream job, but it left him with a lot of time on his hands in Oxford. That would have been a great thing if I didn't have to study day and night. He had been right—my law degree made our lives completely out of sync. At least we had our wedding to plan together, though I had mixed feelings about that too. We had not been out of step since meeting and falling in love—all in the same evening—six years earlier.

I unlocked the door and dragged my bike into the entryway. Then, without even taking my academic gown off, I dropped my backpack onto the floor, kicked my shoes off, and fell back onto the couch. I opened the cover of my magazine, eager to peruse the photos of Prince William walking around Kensington with his lovely mother, Diana. I hadn't even finished looking at the photos when I fell asleep.

I woke up to Franck's kiss on my forehead. "*Salut, Bébé,*" he said, "I'm glad you slept."

I sat up, my heart racing—something it had started to do a lot since I'd arrived at Oxford. "What time is it?" The curtains weren't shut over the window, and I could see it was already dark outside.

"*Shhhhhhhh.*" Franck tried to coax me back down to a lying position again. "You need to sleep, Laura. *Tu en as besoin.* Is that your gown you're still wearing over your clothes? You must have been exhausted."

"I can't sleep!" I wailed. "There's no time for sleep. I have another essay due in two days for Land Law, and I haven't even begun the reading yet."

Franck just surveyed me with his hands on his hips. "Have you eaten yet?"

I felt my stomach. I hadn't eaten since breakfast. Funny thing was though, since starting at Oxford, I had rarely felt hungry. "No," I admitted.

Franck extracted my arms from the billowing folds of my academic gown and lobbed the gown across the room, where it sank to rest on the floor like a large, black jellyfish.

I shook my head to clear it. I felt like I was coming up from Jules Verne's *Twenty Thousand Leagues Under the Seas.*

"I may have brought you something from France," Franck said.

He had my full attention. "To eat?"

"*Peut-être.*" Maybe.

He got up and went to his duffel bag, which was sitting on one of the chairs around the small, round table. He took out a few things and tucked them under his arm, then walked into the kitchen with his back to me so I couldn't see what they were.

"What—" I began.

"Just wait a second," he said. "Read your *Hello!* magazine."

I glanced over at my backpack, which bulged with the casebooks I needed to start reading for my land law essay. A mental tug-of-war ensued, but in the end I picked up the *Hello!* magazine.

Our flat took on a completely different feel when Franck was there. His presence made me feel safer, even though the feminist in me didn't know what to make of that fact. It also made me feel guilty. Guilty for needing to work so much. Guilty for hating the study of law so much, yet being unwilling to quit.

I had just finished the Prince William article when Franck emerged from the kitchen, the largest wooden cutting board we owned balanced in his hands. He set it down on the marble-topped coffee table in front of me. The flat had come furnished, as the huge majority of rental accommodations in Oxford did. It wasn't exactly our style, but as I had zero time or money for furniture shopping, I was just grateful for what was there.

On the cutting board were *saucisson sec* cut into paper-thin slices, rounds of fresh baguette, and cubes of Comté cheese.

I reached for a slice of *saucisson*, and Franck put his hand over mine, stilling it. "Wait."

He disappeared into the kitchen again and then reappeared seconds later with a bottle of white wine and two partially filled glasses. "It's not as chilled as it should be," he said, "but it will do. I bought it chez Glantenet in Magny. I bumped into Monsieur Glantenet at the bakery, and he invited me for a tasting. We ended up doing a vertical tasting, staying in the same appellation but tasting six different chronological vintages. *Fascinante.*"

"What's a vertical tasting?" I had spent a lot of time in wine cellars in Burgundy, but I'd never heard that term before.

I took a sip and let the buttery white wine rest on my tongue for a few seconds before swallowing. It was wonderful that, now that we were in England, Franck could get back and forth to his beloved Burgundy more often. Still, part of me was jealous about that—a part of me that I wasn't proud of. I didn't want to be sitting in the law library, day and night, searching for obscure cases in ancient casebooks. I wanted to be in Burgundy doing vertical tastings too.

I popped a round of *saucisson* into my mouth, enjoying the burst of garlic and perfectly cured meat and delicate herbs. "Chez Batteaut?" I guessed, naming our favorite *charcutier* near Franck's home in Beaune.

He nodded. "I thought you'd appreciate it."

I leaned over and gave him a kiss. "I do."

Franck took a cube of Comté and settled back on the couch. He watched me as I ate. "You look exhausted."

I tried to summon up indignation but couldn't find any. It was true. "I think this is just my face now," I sighed.

Franck peered down his straight nose at me. "I disagree. I think you're working yourself far too hard."

"That's part of the deal of being an Oxford student." I shrugged. "I just have to buckle down and maybe organize myself better—"

"How could you possibly organize yourself any better?" Franck demanded. "You're working day and night as it is."

"I'm sure I could be more efficient. Maybe once I get a better grasp on how to synthesize the cases…"

Franck frowned, clearly skeptical.

"I just need to get up to speed."

Franck sipped his wine, watching me. "You know, Laura, you *can* quit. It's not going to alter the universe if you decide that this degree isn't right for you."

I stared at the brown carpet, a practical but rather depressing choice for the floor. "I can't quit."

"Why not?"

"I just…can't. I'm not a quitter. I wasn't brought up to be a quitter. Everyone would think I was crazy if I gave up. I mean, this is *Oxford*."

Franck rolled his eyes. "Who cares what people think? It's your life. I don't care if you have a degree from Oxford or not."

I knew that, but what I couldn't make Franck understand was that everyone I had grown up with and, as a consequence, I as well *did* care about prestigious degrees and achievement. The fact that Franck didn't care was a blessed relief, but he was in the vast minority. "I know that," I said, "but I still can't quit."

I could tell from the twist of Franck's mouth that he was frustrated with my stubbornness. We sat like that on the couch for a while, each stuck in our radically opposing world views. Franck broke the stalemate by reaching over and caressing the nape of my neck. I could feel myself melting and leaned back against his fingers.

"Did you do any wedding stuff when you were in Burgundy?" I asked. The wedding was more or less neutral ground. Perhaps because I was so far removed from the planning due to sheer lack of time, I couldn't even keep track of what Franck was doing.

"I looked at churches. Remember I told you on the phone two days ago?"

"Oh yeah," I murmured, entranced by the delicious pressure of Franck's fingers against the nape of my neck. "I guess I forgot…"

"They've just renovated the little Roman church in Magny-les-Villers. New stucco, and they've restored the beautiful old door. It's simple and small, but full of charm. It has those beautiful old flagstones you love so much."

"Sounds perfect. Can we book it?"

"I phoned the priest responsible for the *paroisse*. I don't know him, but he seemed to think we could have it. He'll also perform the ceremony."

For a wedding to be legal in France, there had to be a civil ceremony—a remnant of the French revolution—at the local mayor's office. The huge majority of French people also had a traditional church ceremony because, just like in Franck's case, they had been brought up in the Catholic religion, and for them bypassing that step was unthinkable.

"The fifth of July is going to come fast."

"It is," Franck agreed, still lulling me into bliss with his touch. "And you still don't have a dress."

I let out an indistinguishable sound that was part sigh, part groan.

Finding a wedding dress was a project I dreaded. As a curvy five-foot-four, I was a far cry from one of those women who could walk into a bridal store and step into ten different dresses that looked elegant and lovely on them. I was still traumatized from my high school grad dress. I had tried on a sample dress in a subtle dusty pink color, and three days before the graduation my actual dress arrived—several sizes larger and the color of a chewed wad of Bazooka bubble gum. I felt like a pink blob all night. Since then, the mere idea of fancy dresses made my skin prickle as if I were about to break out in hives.

Besides, I had read, in the slim selection of bridal magazines that I had managed to flip through in between studying for my torts exam and trying to figure out the intricacies of easements, that it was essential to go bridal dress shopping with female relatives and/or your best girlfriends. The groom was not supposed to set eyes on the gown until the bride swept down the aisle.

My mother and sisters were back in Canada. I had made a few acquaintances who were, I hoped, becoming friends, but nobody who I was ready to take dress shopping yet. Franck was my best friend, yet he was the one person who wasn't supposed to see the dress. This was a conundrum that I simply didn't feel I had the mental powers to resolve, at least not until my land law essay was handed in.

"You need to start looking." Franck pointed to my standard-issue Ede & Ravenscroft undergraduate gown a few feet away on the floor. "Unless you are planning on wearing that for the wedding."

Before arriving in Oxford, I had always imagined the academic gowns were made of some noble material such as silk. They were in fact thick polyester. "Tempting, but no."

Franck took the empty glass from my hand and set it on the table. "Come on. Let's go to bed."

"I can't," I groaned. "If I don't start in on my reading for my next tutorial, I'll never get through it."

"Remember, Laura? Sleep? Humans are not programmed to go without it."

"You go to bed," I said, leaning over to give him a kiss. "I just need

28

to get a toehold in my reading list. I promise I'll be up in an hour or two."

Franck frowned at me but got up. "Should I leave you the food?"

"Yes. Thank you and...sorry," I said. Since I'd arrived at Oxford, I felt as if I were apologizing all the time—for my distractedness, for my fatigue, for my need to work all the time. Was this a good juncture to begin a marriage?

Franck grabbed his duffel bag off the chair. "I hope it's worth it." I heard him mutter as he headed up the stairs.

I sighed and moved my exhausted limbs over to the kitchen table, where I opened my backpack and spread out my ten or so casebooks. Every cell in my body rebelled at the idea of plunging into more cases.

I grabbed a few sheets of looseleaf papers and my endless reading list and, digging deep, opened up the first casebook to find the case Tulk v. Moxhay (1848), which I needed to start with.

This had better be worth it.

CHAPTER 5

That Friday, I slammed open the door to our flat and shouted, "Done!" before I'd even rolled my bike into the vestibule. Franck came down the stairs and wrapped me in a hug.

"Did he like it?"

"Not really," I said. Part of Oxford's traditions was having to read our weekly essays out loud to our tutors in front of the two or three other students who shared a tutorial with us, then having it promptly ripped to shreds by the teacher (or tutor, because everything had to have a different name at Oxford). I had exited my first few tutorials rigid with mortification, but since then I had become inured to the constant stream of criticism and now accepted it as part of the whole Oxford experience.

"He mocked my pronunciation," I added, as Franck and I walked into the kitchen to see what was in the fridge for lunch.

"Again?"

"Yeah. He says I don't pronounce 'controversy' properly, even though if you counted per capita how many people pronounce 'controversy' with the emphasis on the first syllable, I think the North American way would win." I shrugged. "Anyway, who cares? Let the Brits think they are superior. No skin off my nose. My tutorials are done for the week."

"When is your next one?"

Part of me was always amazed that Franck hadn't memorized my tutorial schedule as I had. I knew that I was far from being the center of the universe, but my tutorials governed my life during term time—my entire universe was organized around them. It seemed strange that anyone lived in an alternate universe where they really didn't matter much, if at all.

"Tuesday." I grabbed an apple from the fridge.

"How about we go to London tomorrow and look for a wedding dress?"

"I can't," I sputtered. "I have to go to the law library and exchange the casebooks I have right now and look up all the ones I'll need for my Tuesday essay. There's no way I can take all of Saturday off."

"Too bad," Franck said. "I'm kidnapping you."

"You're not even supposed to see my dress!"

"I'll close my eyes."

"But—"

"I'm kidnapping you. Get used to the idea."

My mind whirred with the impossibility of getting all my work done if I went to London the next day. Still, I desperately wanted a day with Franck, even if it was doing something tortuous like trying on unflattering wedding dresses. I had given him so little of me since arriving in England.

"*D'accord*," I agreed.

Franck's eyebrows shot up. He was clearly not anticipating such a quick capitulation.

"I have a hard time believing I'm going to find a dress that won't make me feel like I'm wrapped in cotton candy when I walk down the aisle." I picked up two wedding magazines from the pile I had stashed, and ignored, beside the couch. "I love the *idea* of a beautiful wedding dress, but I don't believe in the *reality* of a wedding dress that will be beautiful on me."

I sat down on the couch and flipped to the page with a number of London addresses for bridal shops.

The next morning, we took the train and got off at Paddington station. The first store I planned to hit was the Virgin Bride flagship location just off Piccadilly Circus.

"Virgin Bride," I said, as Franck and I walked hand in hand up Regent Street, "now there's an old-fashioned notion." I was certain that Richard Branson, owner of the mega-corporation Virgin Group, appreciated that ironic double entendre of the name of his new chain of bridal shops.

We stopped in front of a massive window filled with mannequins in a myriad of white dresses, all of them looking as skinny and tall as giraffes and as if they were best friends with Vivienne Westwood. I took an involuntary step back.

"We're going in." Franck took my hand in his and dragged me over the threshold. The interior of the shop was also blindingly white, the only color being the words "Virgin Bride" slashed across the back wall in red graffiti lettering.

An hour later I walked out, more disheartened than ever. The saleswoman had been friendly enough but seemed stumped by me when I said I wanted something simple, elegant, but a little bohemian. She had shown me about twenty dresses, but none of them even tempted me enough to take my clothes off and try them on. They were all too pristinely white, or totally strapless, or puffy.

"Don't give up," Franck said bracingly as we stepped out into the cold February day. "Where is number two on your list?"

I inspected my map. "Somewhere called Elizabeth Street. We may as well take the tube."

We exited in Belgravia—an extremely wealthy, quaint neighborhood of London. I checked my magazine list again. It showed the shop we were looking for sold dresses in most budget ranges, but seeing the gorgeous boutiques on either side of the street made this difficult for me to believe.

We had just turned the corner on to Elizabeth Street when a police car came hurtling around the corner with its lights flashing, followed by a second police car, then a third. I scanned the street for masked robbers or some other plausible explanation for the excitement. The frantic pace of the cars seemed so out of sync with the sedate ethos of the area.

Franck and I stopped in our tracks and watched a massive black limousine with tinted windows lumber around the corner. Small Union Jack flags flew from the two front corners.

The limousine pulled in front of a storefront covered in shiny black paint except for the words "Philip Treacy" in gold lettering on the front.

"Philip Treacy!" I pointed at the store. "That's the guy that makes all the hats for the royal family."

Franck turned to me, a question in his eyes.

"All those *Hello!* magazines I've been rewarding myself with after tutorials." I tapped my temple with my finger. "Important research."

"Ah."

"It must be someone famous." I pulled Franck closer.

A burly man with a radio wire in his ear who had emerged from the SUV opened the limousine door. An elderly woman wearing a mauve suit got out. She was a little hunched over, but still she had a certain way of bearing her head, a defiant tilt of the chin despite what looked like advanced years. Her hair puffed up inches above her head in a gravity-defying style.

"Oh my God." A passerby gasped. "That's Maggie Thatcher."

I peered closer. The hair. Of course it was Margaret Thatcher. A slim man came out of the shop and extended his arm to her and ushered her inside. Perhaps Phillip Treacy himself? Before she disappeared inside, she turned around to the small crowd of us that had gathered on the opposite side of the street and gave us a cheeky smile and a jaunty wave.

The shiny door closed behind her. "Wow," I said, "that was a London moment."

"Can't say I was ever a big fan of her politics," Franck said. He wouldn't be, coming from a long line of socialists and anarchists.

As it turned out, the bridal shop we were looking for was just two stores up from where we were standing. It was about one twentieth the size of Virgin Brides, with a cream–and–gray storefront, all understated elegance instead of a brash in-your-face shout.

Inside, a reassuringly mousy assistant came over and promptly asked if she could assist me. I explained what I was looking for, and she led us around the store, showing me several dresses, which, surprisingly, didn't make me cringe. In fact, a few of them didn't make me cringe to the point that I actually considered trying them on.

The woman tugged her limp ponytail, her eyes frequently flitting to Franck. "Is this your friend?" she asked.

"This is my fiancé," I clarified.

"But your fiancé is not even supposed to *see* the dress, let alone help you pick it out." Clearly this woman was used to abiding by proper wedding etiquette. She pointed at a plush armchair stationed near the front of the store, well out of view of the change rooms.

Choosing my dress was one of the few wedding-related things we could do together, and I wasn't going to be bullied into giving that up. "The dress isn't just for me, it's for him too," I said. "I want him to help me choose."

"But that just isn't *done*," she insisted. "I'm worried you'll regret it. Surely you must have a friend."

"My fiancé *is* my best friend," I said. "That's another reason why he's helping me choose."

Her lips drew together in a hard, tight line. "This is all very unconventional."

I liked the sound of that, actually. *Unconventional. Our engagement in Kathmandu was unconventional. Our rings are unconventional...*

"Yes," I agreed sanguinely. "We're unconventional. I think I'd like to try on that cream one first. The one with the lace and beaded bodice."

It was made of raw silk the color of rich cream, with a simple flared skirt only slightly longer in the back (no Lady Diana train for me), which gently curved up my waist. The bodice was constructed of lace and beads, and revealed my collarbones and a bit of cleavage but covered my upper arms. It was simple and exquisitely made.

I ventured out of the dressing room. The shop assistant had to pin it together at the back because it was only a sample dress and too small for me.

Franck was sitting on a green brocade chair, his eyes attentive.

"I don't feel like a puffball." I marveled at my reflection in the three-way mirror.

"That's it." Franck's gaze was so riveted on me that I felt a flush rise up my throat. "That's the dress." I was usually the one in the couple who had an easier time making decisions, but Franck seemed certain.

"I think you're right."

The assistant watched us, frowning still, but proceeded to take measurements every which way to Sunday so my dress would be made to fit me perfectly. She emphasized, however, that proper undergarments were *de riguer* with this style of dress—a normal bra couldn't be worn because the shoulders dipped too low, as did the back.

"You need to be fitted for a proper corset," she said.

"Where can I do that?" I grabbed my notebook and a pencil from my purse.

"Rigby & Peller. They fit the royal family with all of their undergarments."

I felt the blood drain from my face. Was I going to have to be rigged up in some sort of control top nightmare like the Queen Mother surely wore?

"All of the best-dressed ladies in London buy their foundation garments at Rigby & Peller," she continued. "Go to the shop right beside Harrods."

We arranged for her to call me in Oxford when my dress arrived, and set out for the store where the Queen bought her underwear.

Harrods was impossible to miss and dwarfed the Rigby & Peller boutique. Inside the shop were women of all ages being bossed around by matronly schoolmistress types dressed in sober gray, with measuring tapes around their necks. One came up to me and demanded what I needed. I passed her the business card of my helper at the bridal shop and explained that she had sent me there for proper foundation garments.

She nodded briskly at me. "You. Come with me." She pointed imperiously to eight red velvet chairs that were lined up on the far wall of the shop, half of which were occupied by an assortment of bored-looking husbands, one of whom was actually wearing a seersucker suit.

"You. Sit!" she ordered Franck.

She ushered me to the back of the shop and into one of the dressing rooms enclosed with a curtain. "Top and bra off please," she said before whisking the curtain closed behind her. "I will be waiting here. Tell me when you are ready to be measured."

It went without saying that I would not dare to dawdle, or refuse to take off my clothes. It felt strangely similar to a visit to the doctor's office. I wondered, as I stripped off my clothes, if the British didn't secretly love being bossed around.

"Done," I said. "I mean, I'm ready."

She came in and eyed my chest with a calculating stare. "Just as I thought," she declared and proceeded to wrap the chilly measuring tape around my torso just underneath my breasts. "You have a small ribcage in proportion to your cup size. I imagine you have been wearing incorrectly sized undergarments." She clucked her tongue.

I made a non-committal sound of agreement, wondering if the saleswomen there treated the Queen and the Queen Mother with the same schoolmarm officiousness.

"Tell me about your dress," she said while continuing to measure me. I gave a brief description of the slightly-off-the-shoulder and low-backed style, as well as the nipped-in waist.

"You will need a corset," she said.

"That's what the saleswoman at the bridal shop recommended."

"Wait here," she said. "Don't bother getting dressed."

I wrapped my arms around my torso. It wouldn't have been remiss to turn up the heat a bit in the shop.

In under a minute, she returned with a white boned lace corset with what looked like over a hundred tiny hooks running down back of it.

"Turn around," she ordered and whipped the corset around me and proceeded to hook up the back with deft, but cold, fingers. I felt transported into the pages of the regency romances I loved to read.

I noticed there were dangly lacy things hooked to the bottom section of the corset. "What are those for?" I asked, pointing at them.

She paused in her hooking and cast me a strange look. "Why, garters of course. For your stockings. You must wear a silk pair for your wedding, with this corset."

Stockings...a corset... I stared at myself in the mirror. I'd never dreamed of wearing such a garment before, but it in fact suited my curvy figure. I'd never had much luck with clothes shopping, but maybe the problem wasn't me so much as that I had been born in the wrong century.

"Do you want me to select a few pairs of silk stockings in your size?" she asked.

"A few?"

"Stockings get snagged, especially on weddings days," she said.

"Yes. Please."

"There!" She stood up straight again and gave my waist a triumphant pat. She had been right. It could not have fit more perfectly if it had been molded to my body.

I loved the wedding dress I had chosen with Franck, but with surprise I realized that I loved this corset even more. At least Franck would get one surprise on our wedding day—or rather, our wedding night.

CHAPTER 6

"I just got an email from the priest who's going to marry us," Franck said. We were each nursing a pint of Brown-Speckled Hen at the Turf tavern, one of our favorite Oxford pubs tucked away at the end of a narrow brick alley underneath the Bridge of Sighs.

An acquaintance, Peter, was to arrive soon to have a beer with us. We had met in another pub—the Eagle and Child—which was the local hangout for both my college and Peter's college. He was a German doctoral student writing his thesis on some obscure aspect of gynecology in ancient Greece. That would have been a bizarre undertaking in any place but Oxford. I often thought someone should make a book with just the titles of the doctoral theses presented at Oxford.

It was April, yet still wet and cold. Braziers burned outside between the tables, and Franck and I huddled close to one.

"And? What did the email say?"

Franck took a sip of beer. "Apparently it's a bit of a problem that you're not baptized a Catholic."

"You're joking."

"*Non*. Not if we want to get married in a church."

Back in Canada, people often got hitched in fields, on beaches, atop mountains. "I hadn't thought about it much before, but I guess we don't have—"

"We *have* to get married in a church. If I didn't, la Mémé would never forgive me."

I did not relish the idea of disappointing la Mémé – Franck's formidable grandmother. Also, a church—especially the adorable Roman gems that dotted the villages in Burgundy—did provide a ceremonial and spiritual dimension to the mandatory civil ceremony at the Mayor's office. It would be a shame to go without that.

Still, I thought we were done with the strange wedding requirements the French regime imposed on us. Both Franck and I had to get a blood test to deem if our blood types were compatible for procreating. I had to get an AIDS test and a lung x-ray—I still had no clue why I needed the latter.

"So what do we need to do?" I asked.

"It's more what *you* need to do. I'm already baptized, communed, and confirmed a Catholic."

"And the problem is you're marrying a pagan?" I guessed. I wasn't actually a pagan—more like lapsed Anglican—but the French Catholics viewed everyone who was not Roman Catholic as heathens who probably sacrificed goats and virgins in their spare time.

"Yes."

I took a sip of my beer. "Pagan and proud."

"Don't say that to the British priest."

"What British priest?"

"It appears you're going to have to take a few classes on how to be a good Catholic." Franck avoided meeting my eyes.

"You cannot be serious."

"I am."

"You of all people know the last thing I have is time for more lessons."

In fact, the only reason I was out having a beer with Franck was because I had just handed in my last tutorial essay of the week, and was having the evening as a break before heading to the law library again the next morning to start the process all over again.

"I don't think there are tests for this, or essays." He paused. "Actually, I'm not one hundred percent sure."

"How are we going to find a Catholic priest at Oxford?"

"Apparently the priest in Burgundy knows somebody who knows somebody who can set us up with someone here. He's phoning me tomorrow with a name."

"What on earth do you learn in Catholic classes?" I wondered out loud. *Will I be tested on my Hail Marys?* "What did you learn in catechism?"

Franck shrugged. "How to filch the leftover communion wine and drink it on the sly in the vestry. How to flirt with girls from other villages."

"I somehow don't think that is what they are going to want to teach me."

"I'm sure it's just a formality," Franck said. "Don't worry—I'll set it all up."

I was about to say it wasn't the setting up part that I was worried about, but just then Peter came swooping down to sit beside us, three pints in his hands. He still wore his black academic robe—he must have come straight from his tutor's study.

"*Guten Tag,*" he said. "This is my round."

It was impossible to keep up with beer drinking where Peter was concerned. I didn't even try.

"*Bonjour,*" said Franck. "What's new in the world of ancient Greek gynecology?"

"Lots," said Peter. "They've dug up an artifact that could be a speculum or some kind of ceremonial drinking vessel—as yet unsure, but promising."

"I'll drink to that," Franck said and raised his glass.

We all clinked. Afterward, I listened with only half an ear to Peter's exciting hypotheses as I ruminated over how to get the Catholic lessons over with as quickly and as painlessly as possible.

My lessons, as it turned out, were going to be given to me by the Catholic priest, who was somehow attached to a post—I surmised a highly coveted one—at Christ Church college.

I had assumed most of Oxford's colleges were Church of England but hadn't exactly had any spare time to study the ecumenical leanings of Christ Church.

I road my bike up onto the sidewalk outside of Christ Church, the loose flaps of my black gown flying behind me like some sort of ominous plumage.

Not only was I late for our first appointment, but I was battling what threatened to become a full-fledged panic attack. It had begun in my Contract Law tutorial with Mr. Partridge. Something about being closed up in his study, obliged to concentrate on obscure details of verdicts, had triggered sweaty palms, a pounding heart, nausea, and an overwhelming premonition of doom that made me want to escape, even if that meant jumping out the nearest window. I still felt as if I were going to throw up. I was completely tapped out from acting normal in front of Mr. Partridge and my fellow law students. How was I going to act calm for the next hour or so in front of this priest?

Franck, for once in his life, was looking at his watch.

"We're ten minutes late," he said to me as I fumbled with my lock. I bit back a retort. Making it through this meeting seemed impossible in light of my current state of anxiety. I fought back a huge wave of resentment toward Franck and toward the whole Catholic Church in general. Apparently in Franck's world, it was fine to be late for everything except a meeting with a priest.

Once I had secured my bike, Franck hurried to the window at the Porters' Lodge. He told the surly man wearing a black bowler hat that we had a meeting with Father Strawbridge.

The porter grunted something unintelligible at Franck and stepped away from the window. Most of the porters didn't have much time for either Franck's French accent or my North American one. They didn't seem to have much time for the British students either however, so I knew it wasn't personal.

The porter came back and told Franck an office and staircase number and pointed his finger across the flat, green expanse of the Tom Quad with the majestic Tom Tower lording over it all.

We hurried along beside the pristine grass square. I knew Christ Church had been founded in the mid-1550s. How ironic that people even paid attention to time in such a timeless place.

"Do you really care if we're late?" I asked Franck as he chivied me along.

"*Non.*" He said this with such emphasis that of course it meant yes.

I followed Franck up a pale stone staircase. My heart was still pounding, and I wasn't quite feeling steady on my feet. I tried to ponder the mystery of Franck's sudden concern with being on time in order to distract myself.

Franck was not what I would call a practicing Catholic. As he had boasted, he had done the rites of baptism, communion, and confirmation, just as the massive majority of French children had. But as an adult he never went to church services outside of those at Christmas and maybe Easter. He carried an icon of the Virgin Mary in his wallet, but I had always figured that this was just a holdover from his childhood. I knew he had immense confidence in life and was convinced that his grandfather and other guardian angels had rescued him from death several times during his adolescence—such as the time he slid under an eighteen-wheel truck on his friend's borrowed Mobylette and emerged out the other side, unharmed. Still, I didn't think he was that cowed by the Catholic Church in general.

We climbed up to the third floor and then stopped in front of an ornately carved set of doors. Franck knocked.

We heard some movement inside, and the doors opened. The priest was much younger than I had expected. His black hair was cut modishly and styled with gel, and he was wearing black pants and a gray sweater-vest over his priest collar. This was no Friar Tuck.

Franck stuck out his hand. "Father Strawbridge? Franck Germain. This is my fiancée, Laura. We apologize for being late."

Father Strawbridge raised a brow as he took in my doubtlessly disheveled gown. "Tutorial?"

"Contract Law."

"Hellish?"

"Gruesome," I said.

It had been particularly gory, as a matter of fact. While writing my weekly essays, I had thought I understood the concept of Misrepresentation, but as Mr. Partridge picked apart and criticized the logic of my argument, I had the sinking feeling that, in fact, I didn't understand it at all. By the time I left his study, I was not only fending off a panic attack but also feeling like I knew less about contract law after months of tutorials than before beginning my degree.

At one point, as he was dismantling my third paragraph, Mr. Patridge said to me, "You write beautifully, Laura, but the fact of the

43

matter is, your legal arguments are rubbish." I should have felt insulted about that, but funnily enough the compliment about my writing had meant far more to me than the insult to my legal analysis.

That probably warranted more thought at a later date, but right then I had to learn how to become a Catholic.

Father Strawbridge waved us into the room. I tried to act as normal as possible, despite my pounding heart and a dizzy feeling of darkness crowding my vision from the edges.

"Ahhhhhhh…having tutors rip apart my essays…that makes me nostalgic for my days as an undergraduate," he said. "Those were golden years."

At Oxford I often felt as if I were living in the tale of *The Emperor's New Clothes*. There was such a pervasive pressure to believe in the romance of being an undergraduate at one of the world's oldest and most prestigious universities. Yet, for me, the fleeting golden moments, such as sitting at the pub and racing down St. Giles on my bike, were outweighed by the crushing anxiety and the pressure to perform.

Maybe the courses Father Strawbridge had taken were the easy ones. Degrees in Politics, Philosophy, and Economics, formally known as PPE, were referred to by us students as the "Pub, Punting, and Eighths" degree, as everyone doing PPE appeared to swan about quaffing beer, punting down the river, and rowing on the Isis, blithely unconcerned about school work.

Father Strawbridge sat down behind an ornate oak desk, which looked several centuries old, and waved to indicate Franck and I should take the couch across from him. Normally I would have sunk into Franck's side, but somehow this didn't feel like either the time or place, so I perched primly beside him.

Father Strawbridge steepled his fingers. "So. You want to get married in a Catholic church in France. Do I understand correctly?"

The room spun around, and I fought the urge to keel over. To try to get a grip on myself, I concentrated on the peculiar smell of the room—furniture polish and the distant memory of a pipe.

"Yes." My voice came out high and brittle. My lungs felt constricted, and breathing, let alone talking, was an effort.

"Let's start at the beginning. Why did you decide to get married?"

Franck and I looked at one another. I thought back to Kathmandu and how the decision to get married had caught us both by surprise. It wasn't as if we had decided exactly...it just sort of happened.

I cleared my throat. "It just felt right." My answer sounded more like a question. Was this a trick?

The priest merely nodded.

"And because we love each other, of course," I added.

Father Strawbridge nodded again, leaving me feeling frustrated. I felt as if I were back in a tutorial, trying to find the right answer to one of Mr. Partridge's mind-bending contract law questions, and failing miserably.

"Franck?" the Father prompted.

Franck shrugged. "We love each other. Also, to have a huge party."

Oh God. Why did he have to say that? He was so worried about being on time—why didn't he consider editing his thoughts before they just popped out of his mouth in front of the priest?

The Father raised his eyebrows, and I proceeded to squash Franck's toes with my shoe. Of course we were excited by the idea of throwing a party, but that didn't mean Franck had to share that fact.

Father Strawbridge blinked a few times. "A huge party?"

"Of course," Franck continued, pointedly ignoring my foot digging into his calf, "to celebrate our love with our friends and our family in Burgundy. With lots of wonderful wine and food. *Escargots, boeuf Bourguignon, une pièce monteé, jambon persillé—*"

I had to admit my mouth was watering. The food served at the big parties that were traditional rites of passage in Burgundian life— baptisms, communions, confirmations, weddings, funerals—was always delicious.

Father Strawbridge frowned for the first time. "But that's not really what's important, is it? The food and the wine?"

Franck frowned at the priest." Of course the food and wine are important. They are two of the most important things in life."

"But not as important as getting married in the *House of God,*" the priest said, with special emphasis on these last three words.

Answer 'No, of course not,' I telepathed to Franck. *No. Of course not.*

"Well...I suppose you could consider them of equal importance." Franck's tone conveyed a sort of magnanimity, as though he was conceding a point not because he really felt it was true, but because he was feeling generous.

The priest's black brows snapped together, almost meeting each other over his nose. "God is the most important thing in marriage. God *must* be the most important thing."

Franck settled back in his chair and balanced his left foot on his right knee.

Oh no. His debating posture.

"God gave us all the heavenly food and wine we have in Burgundy," he explained. "So we can't really separate food and wine and God, can we? It's all the same thing really. So is love."

The priest leaned forward. "You believe food and wine and love and God are all the same thing?"

"Of course." Franck didn't hesitate.

"Is this what they taught you in Burgundy?"

"Yes. Also, it's just obvious."

Father Strawbridge pointed at Franck. "I have to say I have several issues with—"

"Excuse me." I broke in. "Franck is already a Catholic. That is established. Aren't we here for me? I'm the one who needs to get the dispensation to be married in the church. I have another tutorial in two days, and I need to get to the Bodleian and find the casebooks before it closes."

The Father took a deep breath and seemed to be trying to calm himself down—or maybe he was praying. I glanced at Franck. My fiancé's lips twitched. He was doing a poor job of hiding his amusement.

If I hadn't been so short on time, and if that priest hadn't been the one who would decide if we could get married in a church or not, I would have found it ironic too. I never understood how a celibate Catholic priest could be deemed qualified to counsel a couple on relationships and marriage. Honestly, what could he know about it?

Father Strawbridge collected himself and turned back to me. "You are of course correct, Miss Bradbury," he said. "We can engage in a theological debate at another time. What was your religion growing up?"

Damn. That was a complicated question with a complicated answer. My mother was a non-practicing Anglican. My father considered himself a pantheist. The main belief in our home growing up had been a marked distrust of any and all organized religion. Unlike Franck though, I gave the priest the answer I figured he wanted to hear.

"Anglican," I said. "Church of England."

"Were you baptized?"

"I think so."

"You're not sure?"

"Um. Yes. I was baptized." *I'll have to check on that.*

"First communion?"

"No," I said.

"Confirmation?"

"No."

"Are you willing to convert to Catholicism?"

I didn't want to convert to *anything* really. I just wanted to get married in a Catholic church. "Is that necessary?"

"Not strictly necessary *if* you are indeed baptized in another Christian religion.

I gave him a good-student-listening-attentively nod.

"You must understand that by getting married in a Catholic church by a Catholic priest you are both undertaking an important sacrament. It would help us greatly if you already had a solid base in the Anglican religion, but that does not appear to be the case. Miss Bradbury, you need to understand the differences between Catholicism and Anglicanism, and also understand the gravity of such a solemn ceremony." As he was saying this last part, his gaze shifted pointedly to my husband-to-be.

I nodded with what I hoped was sufficient gravitas to make up for Franck. "I understand."

For the next twenty minutes, we were subjected to an exegesis on transubstantiation versus consubstantiation and how, really, it was simply logical that the wine and wafers served during Holy Communion magically transformed into the real body and blood of Christ.

"Do you have any questions?" the priest finally asked.

Franck opened his mouth but shut it again when I kicked him. Finally I was getting through. I realized with shock that my annoyance with Franck had distracted me from my panic attack.

"None whatsoever," I said.

We made arrangements to meet in a week, which the Father told us would give us sufficient time to reflect on that days' discussion and make some "important decisions." I wasn't quite sure what the

47

"important decisions" were, but it sounded ominous, and Father Strawbridge was definitely significantly less friendly than when we had arrived.

"Yes," I answered, trying to match his gravitas.

He ushered us out, and we waited until we'd reached the bottom of the staircase to speak.

"*Quel débile*," Franck said. "What does he know?"

"What have you gotten us into?" I demanded.

"I'm not sure myself. I've never met a priest like him before. All the priests I know in Burgundy would totally understand about the food and the wine and the party."

"Did it occur to you to just *stop talking*?" I said through gritted teeth.

Franck shrugged. "French people never stop talking. That's admitting defeat."

I looked up at Franck. "I don't know if he is going to give us the piece of paper we need to get married in a church. If you want that piece of paper, you have to either marry a nice Catholic girl or play Father Strawbridge's game. Would that really upset you—if we couldn't get married in a church?"

"Yes. *Bien sûr*. We *have* to get married in a church."

"Then you *have* to play the game." I realized that, because I had been paying such close attention to the altercation between Franck and the priest, my anxiety had calmed down and was now like the ocean after a storm has passed.

This was one of the essential differences between Franck and me. I had been brought up to discern what people wanted to hear and give them exactly that in the majority of situations. For Franck, agreeing with someone was tantamount to conceding defeat, besides being not at all *amusant*.

"Just because I'm not the same type of Catholic as that priest does not mean I'm not a good Catholic," Franck grumbled.

"I know that." I often felt burdened by my Canadian need to be conciliatory and yearned to antagonize people I disliked, just as Franck did on a regular basis. Still, we wouldn't have gotten what we wanted that way—or at least I didn't think we would.

"I have to head to the law library before going home," I said, as I bent to unlock my bike.

"Can I convince you to stop for a beer at the Eagle and Child first?"

That pub was close to our flat and Keble College and had been the meeting place where Tolkien and C. S. Lewis and the other members of their "Inklings" group used to quaff their drinks and exchange ideas.

I needed to get to the law library. I also needed to start in on work right away, but I could tell Franck needed to rant a bit more about our meeting with the priest and the prospect of getting married only in the mayor's office of Villers-la-Faye.

If only this damned degree allowed me more time to be more of a partner to Franck—to give him more of myself, more of my brain power, more of my time. In reality it sucked everything out of me. I didn't like the person I was becoming. Anxious. Exhausted. Impatient. The kind of person who would be okay with having just a civil ceremony that would be less to plan and execute because I was so tapped out. I felt like the dreamer and the romantic in me was being starved away. I knew Franck would miss her if she disappeared, and I would miss her even more.

"One pint," I conceded.

CHAPTER 7

It was our last meeting with Father Strawbridge. We had seen him several more times since that unfortunate first visit, and I had sat numbly while he lectured me on various saints and the true nature of the Holy Ghost, which I still couldn't envision as anything different from the cartoon character from *Casper the Friendly Ghost*, which I had grown up watching on Saturday morning cartoons.

It was the final day, when he would sign off that I had been a diligent, or at least compliant, student during his lessons, and I would sign off that I promised to baptize my children and raise them Catholic.

Normally I would have been debating the ethics of such a promise, but that question had taken a backseat to the one overarching worry that consumed every one of my waking moments—I was sure I was pregnant.

I was late. Not just a bit late, but *really* late. I also felt nauseous most of the time. Franck kept reminding me that I had been feeling nauseous pretty much since the first day of my law courses at Oxford, but this time I was sure it was a symptom of pregnancy.

For a change, Franck and I decided to walk to Christ Church instead of biking. Franck wanted to take advantage of the beautiful spring weather, and I needed to clear my head.

As we walked down Saint Aldate's Street toward Christ Church, Franck kept pointing out lilacs and roses to admire, but I paid them scant attention.

What will I do if I'm pregnant? I couldn't handle it right now. I'll never be able to get my work done and have a healthy pregnancy, let alone a newborn. Oxford undergraduate life and pregnancy are completely incompatible.

Franck must have guessed why I was preoccupied, because he asked as we entered the quad at Christ Church, "Would it really be so terrible? A baby. *Our* baby. That would be amazing."

I raged silently at the fact that it had to be the woman who had to go through the physical changes of pregnancy. "It's not that I don't want children," I tried to explain once again. "I do. It's just that I feel like I can't even manage my own life at the moment. The idea of managing a brand new, fragile life as well...it's terrifying. I know I just couldn't do it."

"You wouldn't consider—?"

"No, no," I said hurriedly. "I couldn't do *that* to a child of ours. Even though I believe women should always have that choice, no...*I* couldn't."

Franck breathed an audible sigh of relief. I hadn't realized how he must have been worrying about that possibility.

"I *would* have to drop out of school though."

"Would that be the end of the world?"

So, we're were back to this conflict between us. We always seemed to come back to this.

"It would to me," I said. "I've finished almost half of it. I can't drop out now. All that work would be for nothing. Besides, what would we do to earn money? We would have a baby to feed too. We couldn't just live like a couple of nomads anymore."

"According to my parents, I slept for the first year of my life in a drawer."

"It's not just the sleeping arrangements," I snapped back. "Pregnancy, childbirth, the lack of sleep, needing to look after this helpless little thing all day and all night with no family nearby—"

"We would work it out," Franck said.

I shook my head, exasperated. "Why are you always so sure things are going to work out? Your guardian angels?"

"Yes." Franck's expression was completely serious.

I bit back an angry retort and stormed my way across the quad with Franck hurrying to catch up to me.

When Father Strawbridge opened the door to his study, I was quite certain that Franck and I did not exactly look like the picture of marital harmony. I was still fuming at Franck's assumptions, and he, I was sure, was still frustrated that I couldn't go with the flow more and just have a baby.

Father Strawbridge ushered us into his study, while Franck and I assiduously avoided looking at each other.

"Well," he began, "today shouldn't take long. All we really have to do, Laura, is have you sign these Church documents promising to ensure that your children will be baptized Catholic and brought up in the Catholic faith, as we discussed last time."

I unzipped my backpack with unnecessary ferocity and unearthed a ballpoint pen. "Just tell me where to sign."

"You don't have any concerns? This is a sacred vow you are agreeing to. It should not be entered into lightly. The last time we met you didn't seem quite as...um...convinced."

"I've thought a lot about it," I said. "It's fine. Just tell me where to sign."

The baptism might be happening faster than the priest could have imagined. Also, if I were pregnant now, would my wedding dress still fit? My thoughts catapulted back and forth between planning for a wedding and planning for a potential child.

Father Strawbridge beckoned me over to his desk, and I signed the fancy, embossed documents where he showed me.

I signed the last document, and then we waited while he wrote up the letter and dispensation to pass on to the priest in Burgundy who was going to marry us.

"I congratulate you on the wedding vows that you are soon to undertake," the priest said to us ceremoniously.

I found myself thinking about a baptism though, instead of our wedding. Would we have a boy or a girl? Would it have Franck's almond-shaped eyes? Would it have my thick hair? Out of nowhere I felt a surge of tenderness and love for that child—even though I didn't know if that child was a boy or a girl yet, or if it truly existed.

No matter what, I found myself vowing our baby wouldn't be an inconvenience. Our baby would be loved.

Later that week, as we were packing our suitcases to leave our flat for Burgundy, I thought again about our baby that had turned out, this time anyway, to be a figment of my imagination. I had promised now, in writing, to have our children baptized Catholic. Maybe though, I was really okay with this, and not just because we wanted to be married in a church.

Maybe I wanted my children to believe in guardian angels and feel protected and watched over. It didn't matter if they were watched over by God, the Virgin Mary, the Saints, or deceased family members. The main thing was that they, like Franck, would always have an internal flame burning inside them, telling them that everything was going to be just fine.

CHAPTER 8

Even though it was noon, everything outside the train window was black. The Eurostar dipped deeper down into the tunnel under the English Channel. I peered harder at the words in my book, willing myself to relax. My level of constant anxiety at Oxford was seeping into every area of my life. In the last few weeks at school I'd found I was vibrating with anxiety from morning to night. I had to work to ward off my panic attacks, which came more and more frequently as Trinity term—the final term of the Oxford Academic year—drew to a close.

My concentration was terrible, and even things that would have seemed mildly disconcerting before—like riding on a train into a long, deep tunnel under the sea—now became terrifying. My anxiety skittered around in my brain, searching for something—anything—to latch on to. *What if terrorists decide to blow up the Chunnel? What if I had a panic attack like, right now?* My heart skipped a beat at that and then began pounding. I was so sensitive that even thinking about having a panic attack could trigger one. I felt like a walking bomb myself, one that blew up over and over again. Everything began to feel distant and far away. I had forgotten how to breathe normally. The familiar and awful sense of doom settled over me like a thick shroud.

"You OK?" Franck stood in the aisle beside our seats, holding two cups of coffee. He looked down at my hand on the seat rest. It was shaking.

"Yeah. Just feeling...you know."

I couldn't always hide it from Franck now, and he was getting better at picking up on the subtle cues of my panic.

He passed me my coffee, sat down beside me, and gave me a kiss on the cheek. "Maybe all the wedding stuff will help," he said. "You know—get you thinking about other things besides exams and weekly essays and reading lists and grades."

The pressure to be a high achiever at Oxford became more crushing as my anxiety grew stronger, which made me feel even more inherently defective. It was a vicious circular ride, and I had no idea how to jump off.

I nodded. However, I wasn't, convinced that the wedding planning was going to help. We were to be married on July fifth, in two week's time. Besides choosing my wedding dress and my corset, and going to the requisite fittings, I had done next to nothing for our wedding—and flayed myself regularly with guilt about this fact.

Franck had been the one to secure the church in Magny, arrange for the civil ceremony in Villers-la-Faye, rent the cellar under the streets of nearby Nuits-Saint-Georges for the reception, and meet with the caterers to hammer out the preliminary menu. I had done little more than say a distracted "sure, that sounds great" to all of those things. Now we were getting married, and I couldn't feel farther from the fairy-tale bride that I had dreamed about while playing Barbies when I was little. I was going to try though. Despite what a complete and utter mess I was, I was going to try.

The day after we arrived in Burgundy was chock full of appointments. We drank a quick *café au lait* at Franck's house with his parents who, I was realizing belatedly now that I had finally pulled my nose out of my law books, were intimidated by the idea of hosting my entire family from Canada in a short ten days' time.

"*Merde!*" Franck said as he looked at his notebook filled with the appointment times.

"What?" Mémé asked, chuckling. "What merits a '*merde*'?" She was staying at Franck's house to help us all prepare for the wedding.

"I forgot to phone back the DJ."

Music. I haven't even thought about music. Music at a party was rather important.

"Renée has invited us over for dinner tonight in her new apartment," Michèle said. "Seven thirty."

"That's nice," I said. I meant it. But as much as I wanted to see Renée – Franck's wine, food, and pleasure loving aunt - my head was spinning with the abrupt changing of gears between my Oxford life and the deep end of wedding planning.

"Come on." Franck pushed back his chair and stood, then reached down for me. "We have to go to Beaune and meet with the caterer to confirm everything."

The name of the caterer in Beaune, Lucullus, was derived from the Roman politician whose banquets were so legendary that his name became synonymous with lavish and succulent food. This boded well, I concluded on the drive down through the vineyards. Franck's whole family raved about the excellent reputation of Lucullus. They not only specialized in traditional Burgundian fare executed to perfection, but, Mémé assured us, they also served large portions, which many Burgundians felt was *de rigueur*.

We were welcomed by a hearty Burgundian couple who, I could tell from their solid builds, enjoyed time at the table themselves. We were invited to sit down in green upholstered chairs in front of a large wooden desk, which would have been considered an antique in Canada. The shop itself smelled of meat marinated in red wine. Another good omen.

"It's a pleasure to see you again, Monsieur Germain." The woman took a file from a teetering pile on the desk.

Her husband shook hands with both of us, but then nodded his head toward the back of the storefront, in the direction of all the good smells. "I must get back to the kitchen. I have a *boeuf Bourguignon* for eighty people simmering that won't take kindly to being neglected."

"No. That certainly wouldn't do." Franck laughed and I nodded.

"Now," the woman said, opening our file, "wedding reception in Nuits-Saint-Georges. Traditional Burgundian. Approximately one hundred guests."

"That sounds like us," I said. In two short weeks, we would be entertaining slightly over a hundred guests from France, Canada, and England. My lungs seemed unable to take in air.

"We will begin with the *vin d'honneur*." She took out a piece of paper filled with handwritten notes and poised her pencil above it. I had sort of forgotten about the *vin d'honneur*. This was what the French called the drinks portion of the reception. Many acquaintances were invited to this portion but not to the sit-down dinner afterwards.

"You'll need *gougères*," she said. These were the airy Burgundian cheese puffs that melted on the tongue. "We usually estimate three per person."

"Not for our crowd," Franck said. "Make it at least five."

"But they are large. We are, in fact, known for our large *gougères*."

"I know," Franck said. "That was one of the reasons I picked Lucullus. Still, my family has prodigious appetites, even for Burgundians."

"But there will be cubed *jambon persillé*, as well—"

"I know," Franck said. "Five per person. Trust me."

She shrugged, erased something on her sheet of paper and wrote something new overtop.

"What's after that?" I asked.

She led us into the dinner part of the evening. First, we would each start off with a dozen piping hot *escargots de Bourgogne* with fresh baguette slices to soak up the garlic and parsley butter, *bien sûr*. Then, after a respectable interval, there would be *coq au vin* with a *gratin dauphinois*. Then would come a *trou Normand*—pear sorbet liberally doused with local Pear Williams liquor, which Franck would be sourcing. This would, ostensibly, help us digest to make room for the gargantuan cheese platter that was to follow—Époisses, Soumaintrain, Cîteaux, le Délice de Pommard, Comté, Brillat Savarin, local goat cheeses, and l'Ami du Chambertin. This was my favorite cheese of all time, one I had been introduced to by my first host mother, Madame Beaupre.

"That is a lot of cheese," the woman observed.

"I love cheese," I said. "My family from Canada loves cheese. Let's not stint on the cheese."

She nodded and made another note in our file. "Then there is the dessert…"

"We are going to arrange that next," Franck said. "We are going to chez Legrand for a traditional *pièce montée*."

She nodded approvingly. "Perfect."

"Chocolates with the *café*?" she asked.

"Yes," Franck and I answered in unison, and shared a smile.

"Then the onion soup," she said to Franck, "as we discussed."

Wait a second. "Onion soup?" I said. "Surely there is a mistake. That must come before…" I mentally flipped through the various courses backwards—*café*, chocolates, *pièce montée*, cheese, *coq au vin* and *gratin*, *escargots*. Shouldn't onion soup come before the *escargots*?"

"*Non, non.*" The *dame* shook her head. "In Burgundy, it is traditional to serve onion soup at around three in the morning to nourish the revelers.

"Three in the morning?" I was one of the first of my friends getting married but, from what I had seen, Canadian weddings were rather tame affairs, often taking place either in the morning and finishing with a wedding brunch, or in the evening and finishing around ten o'clock, often earlier.

"Everyone is going to stay until three a.m.?"

"Later than that," Franck assured me. "Until sunrise at least."

Another feast was planned for the day after our wedding day. La Mémé, who had been cooking for well over a month already, was almost single-handedly doing all the food as her gift to us.

"But when do we sleep?" I asked. I thought back to my wedding dress and all those tiny buttons, and to my corset that I had managed to keep hidden from my husband. It would be a shame to waste all that.

"Sleep?"

"Sleep." I sent him a meaningful look.

"I've booked us a hotel room so we can rest for a few hours before the banquet begins at ten thirty on the Sunday, but I intend to be the last one standing at our wedding," he said, a determined flash in his eyes.

I had heard Mémé make the same vow at her eightieth birthday party a few months after meeting Franck, and I had no doubt Franck would fulfill his promise, just as his grandmother had. Still, what about the fairy tale wedding night? It had already been reduced to four hours or so on the following morning.

CHAPTER 9

I recognized Boulangerie Legrand in Nuits-Saint-Georges immediately. It was the one where Madame Beaupre—my first host mother during the exchange year when I experienced Burgundy for the first time—bought her baguettes every day and where she used to buy a special *pâtisserie* for me called a *boucheron*, a pastry made up of layers of meringue and chocolate ganache.

Even though that exchange year had been seven years earlier, I still dreaded running into one of my host families in particular—the Lacanches, the family who had been the most vehemently against my relationship with Franck. I was eventually pushed to make a choice between the Ursus Club—my host for the year—or Franck. I chose Franck. Maybe I was imagining things, but I felt as though the Lacanches had never forgiven me for that.

In an act of concerted diplomacy, I had visited all four families and had tried to make amends during my first Christmas back in Burgundy. But Franck was with me, and a certain awkwardness was palpable.

The Beaupres—my first host family—were the only ones invited to the wedding. They were the ones I had been closest to, and the ones I had been most upset about disappointing. I truly wanted to repair things with them, and I hoped the marriage invitation was interpreted this way.

I didn't run into the Lacanches and the other host families often, but when I did, it was uncomfortable.

The *boulangerie* was busy, as it always was, but we were quickly ushered into a back room where the baking was done. I watched in fascination as two employees deftly assembled fruit tarts with skillful hands, topping the luscious raspberries and strawberries in each completed work of art with a chocolate disc emblazoned with the name of the bakery in gold.

Long pans of baguettes were placed in a huge industrial oven opposite a platter of over a dozen cream puffs—light-as-air *pâte à choux* filled with thick, vanilla-flecked pastry cream, not the inedible industrial whipped "cream" like in those bastardized cream puffs I often found in Canada and England.

"A little tasting?" The baker queried, gesturing toward the platter. Beside the tray sat a binder with plasticized pages, opened to a photo of the most gigantic tower of cream puffs—called the *pièce montée*—I had ever seen in my life.

The baker picked up the tray and held in it front of me, gesturing with a nod for me to choose a cream puff to try.

I picked one, noticing on closer inspection that it was drizzled with thin strands of hardened caramel. These crunched as I bit into them, contrasting with the ethereal puff pastry. Then my teeth hit the vanilla-infused *crème pâtissière* inside. I let out a sound of unmitigated pleasure.

There were many reasons why I was happy to get married in France, not the least of which was that I despised the Canadian tradition of serving fruitcake shellacked with bulletproof fondant icing at weddings. I hated fruitcake—always had, always would. The French wedding tradition of a *pièce montée* was infinitely more appealing and delicious.

"I think my fiancée approves," Franck said to the baker.

"Would you like the traditional tower shape?" the baker asked, then began flipping the pages to show us cream puffs welded together by the spun caramel into a mind-boggling variety of shapes—traditional Burgundian winemaking baskets, a huge wine bottle, rabbits, Easter eggs, the Eiffel Tower, even what I surmised was a large baby, a slightly disturbing idea to say the least. "We can do all these, and more..." he said, pride evident in his flushed face. "Your imagination is the limit!"

"I think we'll just go with the traditional tower," I said. "Many of our guests are coming from Canada, and the tower will be plenty exotic for them." I smiled as I imagined my family tasting the *pièce montée* for the first time. There was nothing I loved more than initiating people I loved into the glories of Burgundian food and wine.

The baker's face looked slightly crestfallen. It was clear he would have vastly preferred a more ambitious structure. A mere tower was probably insulting to his prodigious skills but, repressing his injured pride with a loud sigh, he picked up a notepad and a pencil worn down to a stub. "How many people are invited?"

"Well, there are just over one hundred people at the wedding," Franck said. "But make it for one hundred and fifty."

"The tower may start to get a trifle precarious for transportation," the baker warned.

"We don't have far to go," Franck assured him. "The reception is just in the cellar under la Mairie here in Nuits-Saint-Georges." I hadn't thought about that, but it was true. It was only a mere thirty meters across the road from the bakery.

The man nodded, then wrote some more, conferring with Franck while I eyed the platter of cream puffs on the table. *Are other groups coming in to taste cream puffs as well, or can I snag another one? The French never eat much between meals. Would it be rude to ask?*

The baker broke off after a few minutes. "Please help yourself to another *choux à la crème*." He must have caught me salivating. "I will pack up whatever is left and send them home with you.

"That would be wonderful," I said, and I plucked another puff off the platter and popped it into my mouth.

Franck and the baker made the final arrangements while I ate a third, and then a forth cream puff as unobtrusively as possible. Each one tasted better than the last.

Finally the baker finished his notes and whipped the platter off the table and back into the main part of the bakery. One of the women working at the counter placed all the remaining puffs in a beautiful, gray box, which she then tied up with an artful pink ribbon. She passed it over the counter to me. The baker bid us *adieu* and said to me, with a glint in his eyes, "I'm so gratified that you approve of my *choux, mademoiselle*." He gave me a wink.

Flushed with happiness, I waved good-bye, and was about to turn toward the door when I felt a hand on my shoulder. I spun around. There was Monsieur Lacanche, my third host father, and the one who had disapproved the most stridently of Franck and our relationship. I hadn't forgiven him for being so brutally harsh with me at my last Ursus meeting, or for taking me to task in front of all of my other host fathers minutes before I had to give a huge speech.

On the first trip back to Burgundy, the *apéritif* at the Lacanche's house had been a particularly miserable affair. Although Madame Lacanche had, I believed, tried her best to be conciliatory, no one could have glossed over the stiff and disapproving demeanor of her husband throughout the entire wretched hour before Franck and I made our escape.

"I understand congratulations are in order," he said, his eyes—which always reminded me of a shark—peering down at me. Franck's arm slid protectively around my shoulder.

"Yes," I said, my voice taking on a fake bravado. "We're getting married."

"I heard from the Beaupres," he said. "The news quite hijacked our last Ursus meeting."

How I would have loved to have been a fly on the wall for that discussion. Triumph bubbled inside me. *So you see,* I wanted to say, *you were wrong. Franck and I weren't just some adolescent infatuation.*

"When is the ceremony?" he asked.

This is awkward. We haven't invited the Lacanches.

"It is on July fifth," Franck said. "We would be delighted if you could come to the ceremony and *vin d'honneur."*

Which was ruder? Not inviting them or inviting them at the last minute like this? Please say no. The last thing I needed was Monsieur Lacanche's disapproving stare on my wedding day.

"Where and when?" he asked, slanting me a triumphant look.

Franck proceeded to give him the details, while I boiled with rage. *How could Franck do that without asking me first?*

After taking leave of Monsieur Lacanche, I stalked across the cobblestoned main street to the car, seething. Franck cast me a glance. The *beffroi*—an ancient bell tower built in the early 1600s, located in the middle of Nuits Saint-George's main street—chimed.

"Do you want to grab a *café?"* he asked.

"*Non.* I want to get out of Nuits-Saint-Georges." *Did he really think I would be happy about his spontaneous invitation?*

"What was I to do?" he asked as he opened my car door. "He knew we were getting married. A few people, more or less, at the *vin d'honneur* is no problem. Remember all those *gougères* we ordered at Lucullus?"

Unbelievable. Franck thought I was worried about a potential food shortage? "You could have just kept your mouth closed and *not* invited him."

Franck got in his side of the car and closed the door. Now, nobody could hear us.

"I don't need the stress of knowing that man is at my wedding, looking down his nose at me to remind me what a disappointment I was to him and the whole Ursus Club."

Franck blinked like a deer caught in the headlights. "But you were right," he said. "We stayed together. We love each other. We are getting married. He was wrong."

I still didn't want him at my wedding. My ongoing anxiety made me feel extremely vulnerable. I didn't feel up to a face-off with Monsieur Lacanche. "I don't need *anybody* disapproving at our wedding."

"Why do you even care what he thinks? He has no importance in your life at all anymore."

"I just don't need the awkwardness." I felt like such an emotional mess as it was, from all the emotions roiling inside me. I didn't need any exterior forces adding to that. I honestly didn't know how much more I could take without crumbling.

"Do you regret the decision you made of choosing me over the Ursus Club?"

"Of course not."

"So…?"

I would have made the same decision one million times over, yet I was still unnerved, even all those years later, that I'd had to disappoint so many people in doing so.

"There will be at least one hundred and fifty people at the *vin d'honneur*," Franck said. "You won't even see the Lacanches. It was the polite thing to do."

It was the *Burgundian* thing to do he meant, the pathological Burgundian need to be hospitable.

While Franck drove past the vineyards toward Chaux, I twisted the pink ribbon of the pastry box around my fingers.

I tried to push down the unpleasant sensation of being overwhelmed, and also guilty for taking it out on Franck and for feeling so anxious about my own wedding. I felt defective—a thousand miles away from the dreamy brides in the magazines I had been flipping through for the past eight months. Franck deserved better than a bride who was barely holding it together.

Without warning, I found myself stranded in the middle of a terrible ocean of anxiety. I recognized the horrible lurching sensation of a panic attack—as if I were trapped in that moment between tripping and falling. Everything seemed impossible, and I could hear the pulse pound in my neck. Every breath was a concerted effort, and my mind filled with terrible premonitions of doom so all-encompassing that they invaded the DNA in every one of my cells. I was going crazy, or I was going to die. Those were the only two possible outcomes.

I wanted to run and hide—to be alone. Even in the midst of my panic, I could still feel shame. Why was I like this? I wondered for the thousandth time.

Oh God. I had to act normal in front of Franck's family when we got home. I had no idea how to act normal when, in fact, I felt as though my very self was disintegrating.

I dug my nails into my palms. *Act normal. Act normal. Act like a normal, excited bride...* Maybe if I played the role enough times it would come true.

We passed into the village of Villers-la-Faye, but I had been so wrapped up in my tornado of thoughts and dealing with the frightening sensations that accompanied them, I hadn't even noticed we were getting close.

Come on, Laura, pull it together, I said sternly to myself. *You cannot be like this.* My shaking hands didn't agree.

I got out of the car and noticed Franck was watching me. I wished he wasn't. When I felt like this, I didn't want to be around anybody at all. Though once I was alone, I felt even more terrified by my thoughts and physical sensations.

"Are you truly that angry with me?" Franck said.

Is that what he thinks was going on? That I was trembling from anger? I untwisted the ribbon from around my fingers, which were taking on a bluish hue. Monsieur Lacanche had actually been completely forgotten in the wake of my panic. I opened my mouth but couldn't seem to formulate an answer.

Franck came over and wrapped me in his arms. "I just felt that all of that was such ancient history, so what did it serve to be impolite? I don't know. Maybe I liked the idea of coming full circle with Monsieur Lacanche. I mean, at that final Ursus meeting, he was so awful to you for choosing me over them, there's kind of a beautiful completion in inviting him to our wedding. Isn't there?"

I inhaled the warm, familiar smell of him and nodded against his chest. My heart was still beating fast, but the tide of the panic attack had receded slightly.

It was so frustrating. Every time I was in the middle of a panic attack, I felt as if any other way of being didn't exist. And yet, when it had passed, I could no more conjure up the acute discomfort and terror of the experience any more than I could remember what it felt like to be born.

It always left me, however, with a limp feeling, as if I just didn't have the capacity to take anything on. And there I was with my wedding mere days away and my family and friends arriving imminently.

I noticed the box in my lap and smiled to myself. I still had the cream puffs. All was not lost.

CHAPTER 10

"Can you believe your family is arriving tomorrow?" Franck asked me as we snuggled under our duvet under the eaves in his parents' house.

"*Non.* It seems surreal," I said. Indeed, my parents, my two sisters, my brother-in-law, and my aunt Sharon were all flying to France at that very moment. They were probably somewhere over Baffin Island, I calculated. They were going to take the train down from Paris Charles de Gaulle Airport to Dijon, where Franck and his father were going to pick them up in two cars. There wasn't room for me, which maybe wasn't a bad thing because they were being picked up at eight o'clock in the morning.

Franck must have been quiet when he left the bedroom, because when I woke up there was no sign of him. I threw some clothes on and went downstairs to the kitchen, where Michèle was sitting at the table reading a dog-eared copy of *Reveries of the Solitary Walker* by Rousseau and sipping on a large bowl of coffee. I gave her the morning *bises* and grabbed an empty bowl out of the cupboard. I looked up at the clock hanging on the rock wall of the kitchen. Eight fifteen.

Just as I had begun to wonder where Mémé had gone—she was always up at about 4:30 a.m., just as she had been when she owned the village *boulangerie*—she marched into the kitchen carrying two trays of rising baguettes, which she proceeded to thrust into the oven.

She greeted me warmly and gave me a kiss on each cheek. But she and her daughter Michèle made no eye contact and were ignoring each other's presence with a skill that was truly breath-taking. I must have slept through a fight downstairs. This was not completely uncommon, but I was used to having Franck and André as buffers.

Michèle lowered her book. "Franck called me from the train station and told me that everyone arrived and they are on their way." She cocked an eyebrow. "If they can fit the luggage into the cars, that is."

My family, with the exception of my father, who travelled for business several times a month, were "generous" packers like myself. It was a North American tendency. How were they going to jam my family's luggage into two European sized cars? Also, why had I not thought about this problem before?

"Franck said it may take a while, but I should stop reading and go have a shower and get ready." She closed her book, sparing a glare for Mémé who was bringing me a selection of jams from the cupboard.

An hour or so later, the two cars pulled up outside the gate of Franck's parents' house. There still hadn't been a thaw between Mémé and Michèle, but thanks to my family's lack of French, I wasn't too worried about them noticing anything was amiss.

When I got a closer look at the cars, I marvelled that Franck and André had been able to get everyone back to Villers without causing a major pileup on *la Nationale* from Dijon. They both must have had zero visibility with the suitcases packed to the gunnels.

My younger sister hopped out first. She was only in Grade 10, a full eight years younger than my twenty-five years, and I figured coming to her older sister's wedding in France was both boring and exciting. I was sure she was disappointed there were few other teenagers in Franck's family, but she had told me she wanted to walk through fields of sunflowers and take advantage of the fact that there was no enforced legal drinking age in France.

Next came my older sister, Suzanne, and her husband, Greg. They had been married a few years earlier, one of those rare married couples who had met in high school. Greg was looking rather pale, from either the drive down from Dijon or else from traveling from Canada with my family, or maybe both—I wasn't sure.

My parents and my aunt Sharon—technically she was my father's cousin, but we had adopted her as our aunt many years before—got out of André's car.

My mom swayed on her feet a bit. Like me, she could rarely, if ever, sleep in an airplane, and we both resented the fact that my father and his cousin had inherited their family's ability to catnap wherever and whenever they desired.

"Welcome! Welcome!" I hugged them all and felt the excitement burbling over in myself. Somehow, I realized, up until that point part of me hadn't felt like the wedding preparations were actually real. Then, for the first time, it sank in that I was going to be married in five days.

God. We had so much to do.

After saying *"bonjour"* and doing the obligatory round of *bises* with Michèle and Mémé and Franck's little brother, Emmanuel-Marie, I escorted my family to the B&B we had arranged for them in Magny-les-Villers, right behind the church where we were going to get married.

Magny was a lovely little village, which was just down the dip and up the other side from Villers-la-Faye. Stéphanie, Franck's sister, had recently moved there to live with her boyfriend, Thierry, who was an ambulance driver at the same hospital in Beaune where she was a nurse in the ICU.

The charming couple who owned the rambling stone B&B my family would be staying at was waiting in the cobblestoned courtyard to meet us.

Madame Dufrène, the wife, was wearing a tailored pencil skirt and matching jacket, with a voluminous silk foulard tied around her neck in that chic way that only French women seem able to master.

"She looks bourgeois," I whispered to Franck. "How did a *citadine* like her end up in Magny?" Magny was, as far as I knew, more of a blue-collar village.

Franck chuckled. "Actually, her husband is a former mayor of Magny, and they are both hard-core communists."

"*Non,*" I said, mainly to myself.

In Canada, no one would dare run for political office as a Communist. While socialism was acceptable, communism did not exactly have a palatable public image.

"Yes," Franck insisted, "she was even more rabid about politics than her husband."

I shifted my gaze to Monsieur Dufrène. He wore a neat pair of slacks and an ironed plaid shirt. His beard, though, was white and fashioned into a triangular point, reminiscent of Lenin.

"*Bienvenue!*" Both the Dufrènes approached the cars and insisted on helping my parents and sisters with their luggage. Madame Dufrène proudly showed us the four interconnected bedrooms where they would be sleeping. I was on the lookout for portraits of Trotsky, but spotted none. Instead, it was a charming space done up with a tasteful mix of antiques polished to a high gleam and soft floral fabrics. It was also, I noticed, spotless. I wondered if communists were obsessively clean as a rule.

Once we got my family settled, I went back with Franck to help Michèle, Mémé, and André with lunch.

"Did you know the Dufrènes are communists?" I asked Michèle as she took a tray of André's *gougères* out of the oven. I had to pause to inhale their buttery aroma.

"*Bien sûr,*" she said. "Magny is full of communists, you know."

"It is?" Franck and I were going to be married in a communist village?

"Of course. Villers has always been right wing, and Magny left. That is the way it has always been. Don't worry though, Madame Dufrène is one of the most impeccably clean people I know." This, coming from Michèle who was one of the tidiest people in my world, was saying something.

"Don't worry," Mémé said from the kitchen table, where she was slicing up her freshly baked baguettes. "Politics has little to do with housekeeping skills."

Michèle nodded. Apparently they had made up, or at least agreed to park their disagreement until a more convenient time.

CHAPTER 11

It was quiet when Franck and I pulled into the gravel courtyard of the B&B to pick my family up for lunch.

"Uh oh," I said, having a pretty good idea of where I'd find them, "where are they?" I crept up the ivy-covered stone stairs that led to their rooms.

I peered into the window and saw a human-shaped, inanimate object on every available bed.

I opened the door. "They're sleeping," I whispered the obvious to Franck as he joined me.

"We need to wake them up," Franck said. "Lunch is ready."

I crept into the room while Franck watched through the open door. My aunt and my father and my mother were all creating a symphony of snores. I paused for a moment, then decided my energy was best spent waking up my mom.

I perched on the side of her bed where she was sleeping and gently put my hand on her shoulder.

"What!" She sat up in a panic. Like most mothers, she awoke radiating guilt that she had been sleeping on the job.

"It's time for lunch," I said. "Franck and I came to pick you up, but...well..." I swept my hand over the slumbering masses that filled the room. "I know it feels gross, but it'll be better in the long run if you don't sleep now," I said. "Otherwise you'll never sleep tonight."

My mother nodded and blinked her eyes a few times.

"There's nothing as unpleasant as having to wake up from a jet-lagged sleep," I said.

She nodded blearily and shook my father's form beside her. He groaned.

It took us a good ten minutes to wake everyone up and keep them awake. André had arrived during that time, and I felt like a boot camp drill sergeant trying to shepherd him and everyone else outside into the cars.

Jayne kept going back to the bed, mumbling, "Just lying down for a few seconds," and promptly falling back asleep. She was the last one I managed to get out the door. I closed it firmly behind her.

Thank God the ride between Magny-les-Villers and Villers-la-Faye was so short. Otherwise, I was sure we would have lost a few to slumber en route.

My almost mother-in-law, Michèle, was waiting in the courtyard with an anxious expression on her face. Franck and I were doing everything we could to help her and André, but there was no way around the fact that it was a lot of work.

She welcomed my family again and gave them all *les bises* in the French fashion, with two kisses on alternate cheeks. I chuckled when I heard her welcome my father. His name, Bryan, was pronounced *"brilliant"* in French, I realized. Brilliant. Shiny. Genius. He was looking pretty much like the antithesis of that moniker. He kept blinking, in a rather failed attempt to keep his eyelids from dropping.

We ushered my family into the barn on the opposite side of the pea gravel courtyard of Franck's family home. André and Michèle had created a magical room inside. The three-hundred-year-old or so rock walls were decorated with Burgundian wicker baskets and lovely pieces of antiques, which they had chosen from their vast collection in the attics of the barn. There was a long table set with a bright yellow tablecloth, and the oak beams were lit up by strings of artistically strung fairy lights. It was a shame that Franck's parents didn't like to entertain more, as they certainly had a knack for it.

My family oohed and aahed at the pure rustic Frenchness of the scene, and I sidled up to Michèle to squeeze her arm and tell her again what a beautiful job they had done.

All of a sudden Mémé swept into the room with two baskets heaped full of *gougères* in her arms. No proper meal in Burgundy started without the *apéritif, bien sûr*, as my family was soon going to discover.

Mémé ordered everyone to sit down. I began to translate her instructions, before realizing it was unnecessary. Mémé possessed that particular brand of authority that transcended languages.

André and Franck were put to work pouring everyone *kirs*—the traditional cocktail in that region of France. I had tried one or two *kirs* in Britain and back in Canada, but had quickly abandoned the idea of drinking them anywhere but in Burgundy and my own home. Outside of Burgundy, *kirs* seemed to consist of a drop or two of blackcurrant liquor, called *crème de cassis*, and cheap champagne. Travesty.

In Burgundy, *kir* was *always* a generous one third *crème de cassis*. We used Mémé's favored *supercassis* which was extra dark, creamy, and had a 20-percent alcohol content. Mémé was convinced that her love of *kirs* was the reason why she enjoyed such excellent health.

The other two thirds of a proper Burgundian *kir* was either local *aligoté*—an obscure white grape variety that was typically only found in the Hautes-Côtes villages of the Côte d'Or—or, if things were extra celebratory, Burgundy *crémant* (also referred to as *mousseux*), which is Chardonnay grapes from Burgundy vinified using the same techniques as Champagne.

I eyed the *kirs* André was passing around, trying to predict the effect jet lag, travel fatigue, and the alcoholic punch of my favorite drink would have on my family members.

"Be careful," I warned. "*Kir* goes down like Kool-Aid, but you'll find yourself under the table before you know it."

They all nodded sagely, but eyed their *kirs*.

Just then the door opened again and Franck's aunt Renée burst into the room. She was a substantial, robust woman with a gregarious personality that made her seem ten times larger than she was.

"Tell me I haven't missed the *apéritif*!" she shouted, before opening her arms wide in front of her and shouting "Ahhhhhh! *Bienvenue les Canadiens!*"

"No, no, you haven't," André assured her, then passed her a *kir*. "*Tiens.*"

"*Parfait!*" she declared. "I'm positively parched. "*Santé!*" With this, she raised her glass, then took several large gulps. Michèle and Mémé slipped out now that Renée had things well in hand.

Renée swept off her royal blue cape and hung it on the back of a chair near the door. "Now!" She turned to me. "Have you taught your family how to do the "*ban Bourguignon*" yet?"

"Not yet," I admitted. "They only got here five minutes ago."

"No matter!" she declared. "That must be rectified *toute de suite.* Follow me, everybody!" she added in English, but with a strong French accent. She then launched into the *ban Bourguignon*—the traditional Burgundian drinking, celebrating, and eating song.

Renée was a laudable choirmaster, and after three rounds my family was singing the "la la laaaaas" and clapping their hands almost as confidently as a born Burgundian.

The *gougères* were passed around and the *kirs* were refilled. Nobody seemed inclined to nod off anymore. I noticed my mother's cheeks had become quite rosy compared to her travel-weary pallor when she arrived.

Renée kept the conversation rollicking, and I was constantly translating between my parents and André, Franck's little brother, Emmanuel-Marie, and his sister, Stéphanie.

Michèle and Mémé came back in carrying huge glass bowls of *tabouleh*, which Michèle had made in the North African way with a ton of mint and parsley and lemon, a little bit of *couscous*, and tomatoes. It was one of my favorite dishes, and was perfectly refreshing in the summer heat.

Michèle headed back to the kitchen and then returned with four stacked quiche pans, each containing a homemade quiche. She set them down on the table and explained each one for me so I could translate it for my family. Two quiche Lorraine with bacon cubes and grated emmenthal cheese, a leek and fresh goat cheese quiche, and one with Morbier cheese and spinach.

We passed the salad bowls around, and I made sure that everyone got what they desired on their plate.

I savored the bright, tangy taste of my *tabouleh* and small sliver of the leek and goat cheese quiche. André had chosen a white Hautes-Côtes de Beaune from Villers-la-Faye to accompany the food, and its tart, mineral flavor provided the perfect complement.

I was starving, I realized. I was concerned that my family wouldn't be hungry, as I knew from experience how one's appetite could be temperamental with the nine-hour time difference between Victoria and Villers-la-Faye, but they all seemed to be asking for seconds of everything.

I was too busy translating to have seconds. Franck's family—apart from Renée, whose English was more a matter of enthusiasm and panache than actual fluency—spoke virtually no English, and my family spoke no better than a smattering of French. As I tried to translate, I realized how fast a clip the French conversation rolled along during mealtime. I was barely given a moment to breathe, let alone touch the food on my plate.

My brother-in-law Greg who had always been proficient in French, confessed to me that he could not understand a word of what was being said.

It was true—Franck's family spoke fast and their Burgundian accents compounded the problem. They dragged out on the vowels on many words, and rolled their "r"s with a relish unmatched in other regions of France. I also realized with consternation that while speaking French, we all made liberal use of Burgundian *patois*, some of it so specific to Villers-la-Faye that the slang would not even be understood in Beaune, only ten kilometers away. Words such as "*p'tchot*," "*limpia*," and "*schtite*" would never be found in any Larousse dictionary.

I was struggling with the translation of "*fais pas ton bêtion*," when Mémé came into the room carrying the huge metal pot in which she had been concocting a *blanquette de veau* all morning. Michèle brought up the rear with a large ceramic pot filled with rice.

"This is just a small lunch," Michèle said, shrugging one shoulder as if in apology, then nodding at me to begin translating for my family. "We weren't sure how hungry you would be."

I immediately recognized the dismay in my family's faces. They had thought the quiche and the *tabouleh* was lunch—a mistake I had made several times after first arriving in Burgundy when I was seventeen, but which I no longer made. They must have been stuffed.

Mémé's *blanquette* smelled just as heavenly as I knew it tasted. I had been so busy translating that I'd forgotten to warn them that French lunches were many courses long—even the "short" ones—and that in France a crucial skill was learning how to pace oneself.

Franck collected the plates and took them two by two to Mémé for her to dole out the rice and the tender veal chunks simmered in a creamy sauce.

"Wish me luck," my dad muttered when his heaping dish was placed in front of him. Squat, hand-painted ceramic pots of spicy Dijon mustard were passed around, and we all dug in. The meal was one of Mémé's specialties, and she had outdone herself. The chunks of veal were so tender they fell apart when tapped on by my fork, and the cream sauce was delicately flavored with onion and herbs, and studded with tiny button mushrooms. André served a Marsannay red that was five years old. The delicate pinot complemented the subtle flavors of the *veau* without overpowering them.

I was worried my family would take a nibble or two of the *veau* but mainly leave their plates untouched. It was an unspoken rule in Burgundy that such picky eating was an insult to the chef. I felt a massive surge of affection when I saw them apply themselves to polishing off their plates.

"There's cheese afterwards." I broke off from my translating to warn them in English. "A lot of delicious cheese, and then dessert."

My parents looked slightly stunned, but they were also adopting that serene expression that comes from a long Burgundian meal.

The cheese course was phenomenal—a beautiful Comté; several plugs of goat cheese from the cheese maker two villages over, ranging from fresh and creamy to dry and pungent and covered in gray mold; a Soumaintrain, which was like an extremely large Époisses and stunk like feet, but tasted creamy and rich and was more satisfying than one could ever imagine; and two glass pots of runny *cancoillotte* from the neighboring Jura department of the Franche-Comté region, one garlic-flavored and one plain; plus many more… Michèle, André, and Mémé had clearly taken it to heart when I had told them that my family loved French cheese.

My dad stood.

"Do you want me to show you to the bathroom?" I asked.

"No." He patted his belly. "I thought I might just go for a little walk around the house to try to shake off the food in my stomach and make more room."

I translated this and everyone burst out laughing, and Renée shouted, "Welcome to Burgundy!" then launched into another *ban Bourguignon*.

We decided that I would lead all the Canadians around the block while Franck and André filled the wineglasses from the magnum of Savigny-les-Beaune *Les Guettes* that Renée had brought to accompany the cheese.

When we got outside the gate, my mother clutched my arm. "Oh my God, Laura. How do they do it?"

"Who? Do what?"

"The French people. How can they eat so *much*?"

"No snacking between meals, go easy on the baguette slices, and remember that it's a marathon, not a sprint."

My family nodded and groaned as we trundled up the street past the *boulangerie* and the village church.

When we came back inside and sat down in front of the cheese platter, newly filled baskets of baguette slices, and our fresh glasses of Savigny-les-Beaune, I noticed that Franck was missing.

"Somebody called for him on the phone," Mémé said.

"Who?" I asked.

Mémé merely shrugged, looked at my mother's plate, and then remarked with dismay that she had only served herself five different kinds of cheeses.

"Tell your mother to take more!" Mémé urged me. "She's trying to be polite by not taking too much, but tell her she must taste everything."

I didn't have the heart to inform Mémé that my mother was in fact being polite by taking *any* cheese when she was already stuffed, so I relayed the instructions to my mother. She stared at me with eyes as round as an owl, but obeyed.

When Franck came back into the room, I noticed that his olive complexion had paled by several shades. He sat down at his place on the opposite side of the table, but I beckoned him over to my side.

I turned to him when he came over. "What is it?" I whispered.

"Is it that obvious?"

"Maybe not to everyone. They're probably a bit tipsy by now anyway. But to me, yes."

"I'm not sure I should tell you now—"

I rolled my eyes. "Now you *have* to tell me."

"That was the priest, Father Gaillot."

"I take it he wasn't calling to say that all of our wedding plans were going smoothly?"

Franck shook his head. "Apparently, he has no choice but to cancel our wedding."

No words came, which was fortunate, as anything I would have said would have pulled everyone's attention toward our crisis.

"He can't do that," I finally said.

"He just did. He said he mixed up his calendars and has another 'important' marriage that he needs to officiate in Magny-les-Villers at the same time as ours."

"Magny-les-Villers? But that's our church!" I reached up for his hand and squeezed it until I heard his knuckles crack.

"Not anymore." Franck deftly removed his hand from my grip and massaged his fingers.

"*Le connard!*" I swore, low and vicious. *Another wedding more important than our wedding?* "We booked first, so he can't just bail on us like that…wait…is it because I'm not *Catholic?* I signed that piece of paper."

Franck shook his head. "I think this has much more to do with money and potential donations to the diocese than religion."

"That's revolting."

"I know."

"What are we going to do?" I looked around the table at my family, who appeared full and tipsy and enjoying everything so far. We couldn't tell them that the wedding was *cancelled.*

"I have an idea," Franck said. "There's no need to mention this to your family, not yet anyway. I'm going to go back inside and make another phone call. Can you hold down the fort here while I do that?"

"Of course," I said. "What are—"

"I'll explain later," he said. "Just trust me." He slipped back out again, stealthy as a barn cat.

I turned back to the table, where my father was trying to explain something earnestly to Michèle in his non-existent French. She was nodding, but I could tell that she had absolutely no clue what he was saying. It was interesting that although people's French didn't actually get better the more they drank, their confidence in their French ability certainly did. Michèle turned her head to me and widened her eyes in what looked like a plea for help.

My mind was churning with the possibility of a cancelled wedding, but I forced myself to pay attention. "What were you were trying to say, Dad?"

With that, I was swept into a wave of translation. People had to wait their turn for me to translate, and often I had to cut people off to move on as fairly as possible to the people who were waiting. *Why oh why couldn't my parents have been a little more diligent with the set of BBC French tapes my dad had purchased online?* I needed some quiet where I could think.

On second thought, maybe not being able to think is a blessing…

Franck merely squeezed my shoulder as he passed behind me and then sat down across the table. He sipped his wine instead of helping me translate. He was smiling though. I hoped that was a good sign.

CHAPTER 12

The "lunch" went until seven o'clock that night, as lunches in Burgundy were wont to do. Once we got my family thoroughly fed and drunk, we drove them back to their B&B, where they giggled as they crawled into bed. I had a feeling that none of them would be waking up for a good long while.

"And that"—Franck closed the door firmly behind him—"is how you deal with jetlag in Burgundy."

"Effective," I admitted. "But you have to tell me what happened. Can we get married or not?"

"I tracked down a priest friend of mine from my Lourdes days."

Franck often talked about volunteering in the summer with the diocese in Lourdes, the Catholic pilgrimage spot where the Virgin Mary was said to have appeared before the peasant girl Bernadette in 1858. Franck was a *brancardier,* which meant he ferried the ill and disabled pilgrims around the holy site. He also, it seemed, partied quite extensively in the bars of Lourdes once all of their charges were tucked into their beds for the evening. The Catholics, it appeared, saw no conflict whatsoever in doing God's work during the day and celebrating in devilish style at night. Puritanism, this was not.

"His name is Yves Roux. He's a priest now somewhere in the Saône-et-Loire." That was another department of Burgundy directly below ours.

"Can he perform the ceremony?"

"He can, but he needs to talk to Père Gaillot who cancelled to see if he can get permission to use another church around here. Like it or not, this is Père Gaillot's diocese—it's all ridiculously political."

"Gaillot (out of lack of respect, I had ditched the "Père") can't have any objection to that. After all, he cancelled on us mere days before our wedding, that hypocritical, money grubbing—"

"I know, I know. This is the ugly underbelly of the Catholic Church."

Franck seemed remarkably calm, whereas I felt as if I were going to combust with rage. "Aren't you angry?" I asked in wonderment.

"Of course," Franck said, "but we have five days. We can't waste time being angry. We have a wedding to plan."

"You have a point." I knew that, whereas humdrum everyday life wasn't always well-suited to Franck's aptitudes, there was no one who functioned more effectively in a crisis.

"We have to go to the Saône-et-Loire tomorrow morning to meet with him," Franck said.

"What are we going to do with my family?" I asked.

"They'll want to sleep, right?"

"I suppose so."

"Madame Dufrène will serve them a lovely breakfast at the B&B when they wake up. I think a slow morning is exactly what they need. We'll be there and back before they're even operational."

"Ok." I nodded. "So tomorrow, we're going to go and capture a priest."

It turned out Père Roux wasn't just stationed in the Saône-et-Loire, he was stationed in the *deep* Saône-et-Loire—the department just below Côte d'Or. His diocese comprised of small rural villages that were scattered around the town of Cluny, Franck told me on the way there. Like pretty much everywhere in France, Cluny was steeped in history, having been established as a Benedictine Abbey in 910, and having grown to be a major religious center in Europe in the following centuries.

The hills were more rounded and undulating as we drove south. They were dotted with sheep and white Charolais cows and miniscule little villages built out of a golden shade of stone.

"It's beautiful," I said.

"I don't get here often enough," Franck said, "But I've always found this region stunning."

"Maybe we should move down here." The words popped out of my mouth before I could think twice.

Franck's head turned to me so quickly that the car swerved on the road. "You mean now? You mean you'd quit your law degree?"

I instantly regretted not filtering my thoughts before they had popped out of my mouth. Franck would be delighted if I quit—he had made that quite clear. It wasn't because he didn't want me to succeed, but because he knew me well enough to see how unhappy I was studying law.

I didn't answer right away. "Maybe once I make enough money in London for us to retire," I said, finally.

Franck's fingers tightened on the steering wheel so much that his knuckles turned white. "You mean you are willing to be miserable for years just to buy the possibility to *maybe* be happy once we retire?"

I opened my window. Even though the air conditioning was on, I needed fresh air. "I don't know…I mean, I can't think of any other way. If we came down here, what would we do for work? My spoken French is good, but my written French is appalling. I mean, it would just seem like quitting—like copping out of life."

"I don't see it that way."

"How do you see it?"

"I see it as actually living, compared to what you are doing now. There is no rule that says you have to pay for happiness with misery, you know."

I gnawed my lip. Franck and I just didn't see eye to eye on this. It was a big, looming difference of opinion that had been hovering over us ever since I had applied to law schools. Part of it was our backgrounds, I knew. He was brought up in a family where he was the first person ever to go to University. His parents encouraged education and learning, but they weren't able to give him any more direction beyond that. Now that he had his master's in communication from the Sorbonne, Franck didn't feel like he had to follow any particular path or achieve anything in particular, except reveling in the adventure that was life. Money, career…those were all things he just figured would work themselves out.

I, on the other hand, had been brought up to be practical. My thoughts always leapt to the future and how I could actively strong-arm it into a specific shape. I was taught to always have a plan, and that plan required strategy, hard work, and, above all, *not* quitting. Life without a plan, as Franck seemed to be completely comfortable living, was a foreign concept for me—it seemed impossible and, frankly, flaky. We were adults now. We couldn't just do whatever we felt like and float from one desire to the next.

Planning and working toward goals was how I had been taught to live, whereas for Franck, that was the antithesis of living. How were we ever going to reconcile that?

We pulled into Cluny and parked on a charming curved thoroughfare lined with cafés, *tabacs,* restaurants, and shoe stores devoted to the beautiful French children's shoes that all French youngsters seemed to wear.

The town was animated without being crowded. I checked my watch. It was ten o'clock, and the sun had already begun to scorch. Most people were smart enough to seek shade in their homes or elsewhere, not wander the main street trying find a priest four days before their wedding.

"Where is this café?" I asked, a bit tetchy. The heat wave all the meteorologists had predicted seemed to have arrived. Franck was impervious to the heat, thanks, surely, to his Mediterranean blood. I, on the other hand, thanks to my Scottish and Irish ancestry, felt like I was melting under the oven-like heat of continental Burgundy.

"He said it was somewhere here on the main street," Franck said.

"No more specific than that?" *See? This is what happens when you just float. You wander around without meeting the person you are supposed to meet, come down with heatstroke, and end up with a wedding ceremony with no officiating priest.* The potential for disaster loomed large in my mind. There had to be practical people in life, right? And there had to be at least one practical person in every couple as well. Sometimes though…sometimes it was no fun being the practical one. A part of me, a part I often squashed, yearned to be the one who could coast, who could dream, who could just trust things would turn out okay.

As we walked down the street, sweat dripped down the back of my shirt and behind my knees. I could almost hear the *tick, tick, tick* as my anger neared detonation.

"Ah!" Franck exclaimed and lifted his arm to wave at a husky man who was wearing not a priest's collar but a plaid, short-sleeved dress shirt and khaki shorts. His shirt was wrinkled, and the first few buttons were opened to a hairy expanse of a barrel chest adorned with a large gold cross.

"Bonjour, Yves." Franck shook his hand with a strange mix of both respect and mock ceremony. "What, no collar today?"

This man, aside from the cross, did not look remotely priest-like to me.

"Ugh, you have to be kidding me," he said, a broad, hairy hand creeping to his flushed neck. "I had to wear it this morning for Mass—that was bad enough. And the robes...don't even get me started about the robes in this heat. Polyester does *not* breathe, you know."

"What about hair shirts and all that?" Franck asked, sitting down and gesturing for me to do the same.

"You're confusing me with the Jesuits." A deep, rumbling laugh emanated from Yves's chest. "I'm no Jesuit."

Franck introduced me to the Father Yves Roux. I shook his large, square hand politely, tampering down a spurt of annoyance. I always found it irritating when Franck didn't plan things and things worked out anyway. It shook my certainty, and made me wonder if all my theories about needing to be practical might not be as sound as I needed to believe.

Franck looked around him, smiling. "I think the last time I was in a café with you was in Normandy during that youth group retreat. When was that, about ten years ago?"

"At least." Père Roux nodded. "If I recall, we discovered something called *café*-Calva, and we were both significantly worse for wear." Père Roux let out his distinctive laugh again, which made me warm to him.

"How could I forget?" Franck said. "Do you remember our conversation that night?"

"I remember we got into a discussion where we basically had ourselves convinced we had changed the entire existence of the universe as we know it."

"Then we passed out," Franck said.

Père Roux's impressive shoulders shook with amusement. *"Mon Dieu.* That hangover the next morning…"

I had never heard a priest talk like that, so casual, so approachable, so human. My annoyance fled in the presence of fascination.

"Do you remember Sister Yvette and her *deux-chevaux?*"

"How could I forget?" Franck laughed. "I had to drive up with her all the way from Burgundy to Normandy. She never shifted out of second gear."

"Do you remember the smell of the poor clutch?"

"It's amazing it didn't fall out on the road like a piece of burnt charcoal." Franck signaled to the waiter and asked him to bring us two coffees and two glasses of water.

"So what is this bind you're in?" Père Roux wiped a trickle of sweat from his forehead.

Franck explained how the Père Gaillot bailed on us because of his "more important" wedding, leaving us with both of our families and no priest to conduct our planned ceremony.

"It's *dégueulasse.*" I chimed in. Revolting.

Père Roux nodded. "It is. Of course I'm not technically allowed to say that, but it is. It doesn't surprise me with him, to tell you the truth."

"Can you come and do it?" Franck asked, getting right to the point as usual.

"I'd be glad to, but unfortunately I'll have to get permission from Père Gaillot first."

"I wasn't too polite at the end of our phone call," Franck said, "but I can try to call him back and get permission."

"No, I'll call him," Père Roux said. "It's better if it comes from me. I'll do it this afternoon and call you this evening to let you know."

I let out a *whoosh* of air that I didn't realize I had been holding. I guess the church wedding had become important to me too, and not simply, I suspected, because it was important to Franck.

"There's one other little thing, but I can't see it being a problem," Franck said.

"What?" Père Roux signaled the waiter and ordered a *panaché*—a chilled mix of lager and lemonade.

"Laura's not exactly Catholic."

Père Roux smiled at me. "Not *exactly*?"

"More like, not at all," I admitted. "But when we were at Oxford, we met several times with a priest there—Father Strawbridge—and he gave me some lessons and we did…you know…all the necessary *stuff*."

"Stuff?" Père Roux echoed, not unkindly, but clearly mystified. His *panaché* arrived, and I looked longingly at the beads of condensation on the sides of his tall, cool-looking glass.

"I think I'd like a *panaché* too," I said, before answering. "That looks refreshing."

"Make it two," Franck said. "Good idea."

Père Roux prompted, "So…you were going to explain the 'stuff'?"

"Oh yes. I meant the lessons and the promising to be a good Catholic, and signing the piece of paper about bringing up my children Catholic and having them baptized and all that."

"Ah. *That* stuff."

"Yup."

"And you felt all right about that?"

"I wasn't brought up with any religion in particular, so I'm happy to give my children a grounding in something, even if they choose to reject it later on. Also, Catholicism isn't just a religion in France, it's part of the culture, and any children we have will be half French."

"Oh," Pere Roux said faintly. "Well…that…" His eyes shifted to Franck, who was nodding reassuringly. "Oh," he said again.

"Laura has decided to be honest today," Franck said.

I remembered how I had gotten angry at Franck for doing the exact same thing with Father Strawbridge in Oxford. Yet, there was something about Père Roux that incited candor. *Have I gone too far?*

"I see," Pere Roux said, and I was relieved to see he looked entertained rather than angry. "To be honest with the demographic problem the Catholic Church is facing right now, I am hardly going to start getting picky about who wants to participate and why."

Thankfully, our *panachés* arrived just then. I sipped the perfectly sweet and bitter combination, and sighed. "That hits the spot."

Franck and the Père launched into recounting stories of the youth camps they had attended together.

"Do you remember when we were in Brittany and you realized that we forgot to send in the money to the insurers to cover any accidents on our trip?" Pere Roux said before gulping back the last dregs of *panaché* and wiping off his mouth with the back of his hand.

Franck slapped his thigh. "And Sister Yvette told us not to worry, that God held us all in his hand, and then took us out to that bar that served those huge mugs of cider?"

"Where we spent all of the insurance money." Père Roux laughed. "But she was right. God did take care of all of us. We were all just fine."

"More importantly, nobody ever found out."

I listened in fascination. Père Roux was nothing like any priest I had ever met before. He was irreverent, a *bon vivant*... Was he truly deeply spiritual or was being a priest, I wondered, just something he had decided to do because he couldn't think of anything better?

"And you?" he asked Franck when they had recovered from their last bout of laughing. "Have you been going to church?"

Franck shook his head. "Not much... In Oxford, Laura and I do like to go to services in the different college chapels. Beautiful buildings. Wonderful choirs and music. But most of those are Anglican, not Catholic."

He shrugged. "Better than nothing, but still, the Church needs thinkers like you, Franck. I've always told you that."

"You know that's not me," Franck said. "I prefer to do my thinking by myself, not as part of a group."

The Père shrugged and tossed back the rest of his *panaché*, not seeming offended. "I had to try."

"Thank you so much for trying to help us," I said. "Franck's grandmother would keel over if we weren't married properly in a church."

"What about your family?" Father Roux asked.

I thought about this. Many people in Canada got married in churches, but an equal number got married on beaches or cliff tops or open fields, and nobody ever seemed to feel that this was in any way lacking.

"I don't think they would really mind," I said. "Things are done much differently in Canada. It's much less traditional."

"But *you* want to get married in a church?"

I didn't hesitate. "Yes I do. For Franck, and for Franck's family and, funnily enough, for myself. Somewhere along the line, the idea has become important to me too." I had begun to view our church wedding as a crucial rite of passage—I guess I wanted the traditional as well as the unconventional. "Is that good enough?"

"It's good enough for me," the Père said. "And God too, I daresay."

CHAPTER 13

It seemed a long way indeed to go for a coffee and a *panaché*, but we drove home from Cluny in a much better frame of mind than when we had left that morning.

"He was different than I expected," I said. "Nice." It had to work out. It *had* to. I just couldn't visualize having to tell my family, not to mention Franck's, that the church part of the wedding was cancelled.

"It will," Franck said, certainty in his words.

"What should we do with our Canadians this afternoon?" I wondered out loud.

"I've concocted a little something with Aunt Renée." There was a mischievous smile on Franck's face.

"You did? When?"

"I dropped in to see her three days ago when I was running errands in Beaune. We had a few *kirs* and got to plotting."

"What is it?"

"Do you remember Renée's cousin Suzette who lives in Volnay?"

I did. She was a plump, bespectacled elderly woman, who always wore a flowered-spangled house dress and happened to have inherited some of the best vineyards in Volnay and Pommard's *Premier Cru* appellations. She was a legend in Franck's family due to her prodigious ability to tuck away food and drink with Renée and the cohort of *bon vivants* that they dined with frequently.

Once, she had suffered from some sort of cardiac event during the cheese course of a sumptuous eight-hour meal at her house. As the paramedics carted her off on a stretcher to the ER, Suzette had instructed her guests that they could take their time with the cheese and even open a few extra bottles of wine, but that they had to wait for her before having dessert. After all, it was her favorite—floating island, or *oeufs à la neige*.

Her friends, knowing her tenacity for not abandoning a meal before it was finished, kept themselves busy at her table for three hours, drinking wine while she was getting checked out at the hospital. When she got back home after getting her heart rhythm reset, Suzette sat down and enjoyed her *oeufs à la neige* with a glass of *mousseux*. She had also convinced the three paramedics who drove her home to join them for dessert, and they had all agreed that Suzette's *oeufs à la neige* were the best they'd ever tasted.

"I *love* Suzette." I chuckled.

"Everyone does," Franck agreed. "So, Renée and I have planned a winetasting at her house this afternoon, with an induction ceremony for your family."

"Induction into what?"

"Into Burgundy."

"What exactly does that entail?"

"Renée brought traditional silver Burgudian winetasting cups, called *tastevins*, for everyone. These were attached to the ceremonial yellow-and red-ribbons so they could be hung around the neck."

I started to feel a bit of excitement stir in my chest. "What better way to spend the time waiting for Père Roux's phone call?"

"Exactly."

When we stopped in at the communists' B&B in Magny, before heading back to Villers to check on lunch preparations, I was relieved to find most of my family still sleeping. They had, they told me, been up and down most of the night because of the nine-hour time difference.

We told them about the winetasting planned for after lunch, and they all looked a little green at the idea. I knew, though, that when they got some food, wine, and coffee into their system, the idea would start to have vastly more appeal. As the French often said, *l'appétit vient en mangeant*. The appetite comes with eating. I had found that to be true time and time again, especially in Burgundy.

The huge vat of *coq au vin* Mémé had simmered for lunch was delectable, despite the scorching temperature. The barn had thick stone walls—as wide as one meter in places—which kept the inside blessedly cool. I had first tasted Mémé's *coq au vin* at her eightieth birthday party six years earlier. She hadn't lost her magic touch; this batch was just as good.

I knew, for my family, it seemed strange to always be sitting down to these elaborate two- or three-hour lunches in the middle of the day. But as soon as they each had a glass or two of *kir* in their system, they didn't seem to have any arguments with the program.

To most North Americans, taking such a long break in the middle of the day and devoting it exclusively to the pleasure of good food, good wine, and good conversation was unnatural. I knew because I had struggled with this when I first arrived in Burgundy. To my puritan sensibilities it had seemed an unholy waste of time that could be better spent working, achieving, and striving. I wanted to explain to them how I had learned this in Burgundy with Franck's family, and that the French lunch wasn't a waste of time. In fact, I often thought now it was one of the best possible uses of time. Having them come to that realization themselves though would be far more powerful than me trying to convince them. *Life is short. Pleasure isn't sinful. On the contrary, it is one of the greatest gifts we humans could cultivate and savor.* It occurred to me that my school life at Oxford was lamentably short on pleasure, but that couldn't be a justifiable reason to quit. Or could it?

By the time we got up from the table at two-thirty, my family was in rollicking good humor and becoming adventurous in their attempts to communicate in French.

Franck's aunt Jacqueline and uncle Jean rolled up in their minivan to drink a quick espresso with us and help transport my Canadian clan to the winetasting. They couldn't stay with us at the tasting, though, as they had to visit some of Jean's relatives further south.

Franck's parents elected to stay in Villers and rest for a bit. There was much laughter as everyone else tried to wedge into the van. We sat on each other's laps and the need for seat-belts was waved away by Jean, who commandeered the steering wheel.

We wound our way out of Villers-la-Faye, down through the vineyards and the stunning village of Pernand-Vergelesses perched on a hillside leading down to the lower, Côtes de Beaune vineyards. I gave a thankful nod and wink to the statue of the Virgin Mary above the village. It was where Franck had taken me the day after we first met. Even though I had not converted to Catholicism by a long shot, I believed in the powers of that particular Virgin Mary statue. I believed that she'd had a hand in my relationship with Franck and would continue to silently and serenely weave magic for us.

We passed the medieval fortifications of Beaune, and then bumped along the narrow dirt roads through the vineyards toward Volnay.

We pulled in front of a nondescript stone house in the street just above the *salle des fêtes* of the village, set on a flat section of the hillside that provided a spectacular view over the undulating vineyards stretched out below. Fragrant orange roses climbed in a haphazard way up the wall to the right of the wooden door.

Suzette swung open the door and grabbed everyone's face—one by one—between her soft, plump hands and gave everyone a smacking kiss on both cheeks. La Zette, as everyone called her, was wearing her old-fashioned, owl-like glasses and one of her customary housecoats, which that day was of faded shades of blue. "*Bienvenue!* Come in!" she cried, and led us through her comfortably cluttered house, out the back door, and down a steep, dark set of stone stairs into the cellar beneath the house where Renée was setting out a plate of cubed Comté cheese—the perfect accompaniment to Burgundy's pinots. The cellar was several times larger than the house itself and was filled with barrels as far as the eye could see. Racks and racks of wine bottles disappeared into the distance.

"Can you believe my husband?" Suzette put her hands on her hips as we stood at the bottom of the stairs waiting for the others to gingerly make their way down. "Dying on me and leaving all of this for me to sort out? He didn't even have the good grace to drink enough to make a dent in it before he expired." She brushed a cobweb off her ample bosom. "That's why he died, you know. He didn't drink enough of his own wine. Most of us people from Volnay live to well over one hundred, and that's because we've been drinking Volnay wine from the time we were babies sucking on our bottles."

"Your mothers put wine in your baby bottles?" I said.

"*Bien sûr*," Renée said. "Burgundy wine strengthens the blood, you know, and helps babies sleep through the night."

I bet it does.

"Anyway, I have all this wine here and I can't drink it on my own, so you are doing me a favor, you know," Suzette said.

I laughed. "Trust me. It's *our* pleasure."

La Zette gave my family a thorough tour of her cellars, including barrel tastings with a long glass suction tube known as a *pipette* from several different wines. I was called on to translate. La Zette talked in such rapid-fire French with such an entrenched Burgundian accent—which was peppered with local *patois* that included words that I had never even heard in Villers—that I was fully occupied just trying to keep up with her. Renée pitched in to help from time to time, but her attention was firmly fixed on the wine she was slurping and sloshing around in her mouth as she tried to pin down the exact bouquet of each appellation and vintage.

My family, I noticed after a time, were swaying slightly on their feet.

"So," la Zette said after we had been barrel tasting for a good hour or so, "let's get to the real winetasting now!"

"That *wasn't* the real winetasting?" I whispered, *sotto voce*, to Franck.

"Clearly you do not know la Zette well enough yet."

"I thought we would do it at my kitchen table instead of the cellar, because, you know, I am ancient and I don't like the drafts down here."

I couldn't argue, but it dawned on me that, unless she put a spittoon on the table, there would be nowhere to spit out the wine we would taste in the kitchen. Well, except for the sink, and that would be extremely rude. This meant we had to drink every glass, and my family was already stumbling and giggling as it was. Burgundian hospitality could be a daunting thing at times.

Following la Zette and Renée's commands, we sat around la Zette's kitchen table on the mismatched wooden chairs. Their wood was a deep honey tone, thanks to both the patina of age and years of French *derrières* sliding on and off them.

The table was covered with a Provençal-style oilcloth. The cheery bunches of lavender printed on the tablecloth seemed out of place in such a typically Burgundian home with its accents of dark wood with hints of rusty red.

La Zette plonked five bottles of unlabeled wine in the center of the table and then bustled over to the cupboards to help Renée take out wineglasses.

She gestured for us to sit down and placed a wineglass—a very large wineglass I knew was specially made for tasting red wines—in front of each of us.

She stood at the head of the table and picked up bottles at random, then put them down again, peering at them through the thick lenses of her glasses and occasionally clicking her tongue.

"This one!" she said finally and uncorked one of the dusty bottles with only undecipherable (to me, anyway) markings on it in what looked like chalk. "A 1985 *Clos des Chênes*. One of my favorites."

She proceeded to uncork the bottle with fluid movements that illustrated this was an activity as natural to her as breathing. She poured us each a full glass.

I scanned the kitchen. No spittoon in sight. My aunt Sharon was staring round eyed at the glass in front of her.

"You don't have to drink all of it," I whispered to her in English as I leaned over.

"My problem is that I think I'm going to want to," she whispered back.

La Zette began to swished the wine around in her mouth, making slurping noises that I would have thought were rude if I didn't know better. At my very first Ursus meeting in Burgundy I had sat with a group of men in the wine industry who considered it a sacred duty to initiate me in the fine art of winetasting. Never mind that it was officially against the rules of my student exchange to drink alcohol. I had learned within the first few hours after arriving in France that this rule did not hold water in Burgundy.

I took a sip. I knew 1985 had been a stellar vintage, almost perfect as far as weather and growing conditions went. There was, in fact, little of it left to buy anywhere. Connoisseurs and collectors had snapped it up as soon as it was bottled.

I swirled the wine in my glass and held it up to the light to admire its color and its legs. It was a deep rust, turning to garnet at the top, and its solid, thick rivulets were a thing of beauty. *La Zette's wine has legs.* I took a reverent sip. I tasted first a faint hint of violets, then strawberries, and then, as I let the wine sit on my tongue, blackcurrants. This was all held together with an earthiness and excellent tannins, which kept it from being cloying.

It was an incredible wine. The kind of wine that stopped me in my tracks and robbed me of both my breath and powers of speech. It was wine as a spiritual experience.

"Wow!" Franck said, after a minute or two. "This is phenomenal, Zette."

She nodded. "My husband was a true winemaker. It was in his blood, in his heart. I believe he actually liked his vineyards more than his children, you know, and probably even more than me."

"Did that bother you?" I asked.

"*Non*," she said, taking a moment to suck and swish the wine around her mouth, as all knowledgeable wine tasters knew how to do. "He understood the vines, you see, in a way that he never understood people—even his own family. Besides, winemaking is a noble thing to love and to commit one's life too. He was a true *artiste*."

I wondered at such forbearance. I knew Franck's patience with me pursuing this law degree to the exclusion of everything else was running out. What were his limits? What were mine? I didn't think either of us was as patient as la Zette had been with her husband. Or maybe the difference was I didn't love the law, and Franck knew it.

Another thing niggled at me. I couldn't really call a law degree a noble calling, not in my case at least. Amongst my fellow students were certainly some for whom the law was more a vocation than a career. They lived and breathed notions of justice, change, and helping others. I was jealous of these students, much to my dismay. For the majority, though, a law degree—especially a law degree from Oxford—was merely a path to a prestigious career, lots of money, and a certain lifestyle. They, like me, possessed no burning passion for the law itself.

For the first few weeks at Oxford, I had been waiting for that godly breath of a spiritual awakening to infuse my cells, for fervor for my legal studies to suddenly strike me. It never came, however, and now I was certain it never would. When learning about contracts and important judgments, I just simply couldn't bring myself to care. Yet I *should* have. These were real people's fates being decided by these legal decisions, after all.

Unlike Suzette's husband and his vines, I couldn't lie to myself that I was answering a noble spiritual call, worthy of a multitude of sacrifices. Yet I was asking not only myself but also Franck to sacrifice many things—to have hardly any time together, to have a wife that was an anxious mess most of the time, to put off having babies…

Was it right to marry him in light of all of that? Part of me wanted to wait until my life was less…messy. But I had no idea when that would be. For the moment, I couldn't see a feasible off-ramp for my mental turmoil.

I loved him. And I knew I could promise to always love him. But I worried it wasn't enough.

"Laura!" My aunt Sharon was shaking my forearm, bringing me back to Suzette's kitchen table. "Can you please translate that for me?"

"What? Sorry. I drifted off there for a moment."

"Tell Suzette that I'm a widow too, but all my husband left me, besides memories, was a collection of his homemade hunting knives."

I translated this, and la Zette snorted with laughter and slapped the tabletop with her palm. "They are useless sometimes, aren't they," she said, "these men of ours?"

I translated this as well, and Sharon joined la Zette, breaking out in peals of laughter.

They were both widows. Who knew how long Franck and I had together before one of us shuffled off this mortal coil? *That* was an argument for getting married and figuring this stuff out together, even if it promised to be difficult.

I looked at the glass in my hand. I had somehow consumed all my wine without noticing. It was that good.

"*Alors*, la Zette!" announced Renée in her usual commanding style. "You are sleeping at the wheel. This is not like you, *ma chère*. What are you going to serve us next?"

Surely the next glass will be smaller.

La Zette served my mother first, and she poured a glass that, like the first one, was three-quarters full. My mother's eyes met my eyes, and she cast me a desperate look.

I glanced around the kitchen again. No spittoon, no pea gravel where many people dump their wine during Burgundian winetastings, and which always gave the cellars the seductive smell of wine. I shrugged at my mother in apology. I couldn't figure out a way to bring up the topic without gravely offending Suzette and Renée and their Burgundian hospitality. Burgundians took welcoming others into their home and to showing them a fine time very seriously, which meant they always offered delectable food, sublime wine, and lots of laughter. Suggesting that maybe we didn't want Suzette's incredible wine would be an insult of the highest order. I couldn't do that. Besides, it was truly an honor to drink this wine. My family would just have to suck it up. They were there, I reflected, to earn their status as honorary Burgundians. They were doing exactly that in a way that no other hazing ceremony could accomplish.

The only two people in my family who seemed to find no fault with the program up to then were my sixteen-year-old sister, Jayne, for whom drinking copious amounts of wine with her family was a novel and exciting experience, and my father, for whom Burgundian wines were somewhat of a religious experience. His eyelids had drifted slightly over his eyes and he was sitting back in his chair, his wineglass held in front of him, a magnanimous smile on his lips. I was familiar with that feeling of deep satisfaction with the universe that Burgundy wines could conjure.

La Zette kept serving the wines and we kept drinking them, until finally she shooed Renée and Franck down to the cellar with a wink and a flap of her hand. A few minutes later, she announced for me to translate, "We are preparing a little surprise for you in the cellar. Laura, can you take your family for a little walk around the church while we finish? Come back in about ten minutes. The fresh air will do them good, I'm sure."

La Zette leapt up in a sprightly manner and marched toward the cellar. She seemed absolutely no worse for wear from the wine. The rest of us, however, swayed on our feet and were taken with a sudden attack of the giggles.

"I don't think I've ever drunk that much in one sitting," gasped my sister Suzanne.

"But wasn't it good?" I asked.

"Delicious." My brother-in-law swayed and clutched on to the kitchen table for support.

"What surprise are they planning?" asked Jayne. "Do you know?"

"I have an idea," I said. "But it's a secret. Come on. Let's go try to sober up a tiny bit."

CHAPTER 14

Laughing and bumping into each other, we somehow made our way out the kitchen door. The mid-day heat had subsided, and the temperature was warm without being sweltering. We all took gulps of fresh air and blinked against the bright sunlight.

"Where is the church?" Sharon asked. "Is it far?"

"No." I pointed up the street. "It's thirty feet away."

I led the motley tribe up the curved road from la Zette's doorway to the village church, and we all were highly entertained by our inability to walk in a straight line.

"We're hardly in a fit state for church," said my mother, and then dissolved into laughter after I bumped into her, and then Sharon bumped into me.

A proper-looking woman—certainly British by the sounds of her refined conversation with the man beside her, who was dressed in a suit and tie—was also walking toward the church. She looked askance at us.

"Act sober," hissed my mother. "That snotty lady is looking at us."

"So what?" I asked.

"She looks disapproving."

We tried to adopt a more dignified gait, but we could only pretend for so long. As soon as we had passed her and her gentleman friend, the whole group of us collapsed into each other, some of us having to grab on to the others to keep them from falling to the ground in mirth.

"What a disgrace!" I heard a diamond-sharp British accent behind us. This only made us laugh harder.

We somehow made it into the dimness of Volnay's little Roman stone church.

"Ok guys, listen up," I said. I plucked a brochure from a stand by the door and began translating the history. "This church dates back to the thirteenth century…," I began.

My family all sat down on the benches nearest to the altar to listen to my little history lesson. My father crossed his arms over his chest and settled into a pleasant little catnap. The rest of them stared either off into the middle distance or at the ceiling. They all looked quite beatific, as though they were in a state of profound meditation or religious conversion.

"Ok," I said, after checking my watch, "that's long enough. Let's go back to la Zette's"

They all took their time getting up, as though they were moving through molasses. The giggling began again as they clutched the curled wooden tops of the benches to keep steady.

"Behave yourselves," I said with mock discipline.

"Yes, ma'am." My dad hiccupped.

I led them back out into the sunlight again. We all blinked at a tractor piled high with pruned grape vines, which was turning into a vinter's property with a sign advertising it as Domaine François Buffet.

"Look! That domaine dates back over three centuries." I pointed at the sign. "We'll have to do a tasting there one day."

"Maybe when I sober up," my father quipped. "Like in ten years."

The British couple was still slowly making their way around the church. The woman gave us a dirty look before ducking in Le Cellier Volnaysien, a wonderful restaurant in a huge wine cellar, which had been there for as long as I had been coming to Burgundy, and probably much longer.

We made quite a racket re-entering la Zette's kitchen.

"Where are you?" I hollered, as there was nobody to be seen.

"In the cellar!" Franck's voice came back.

"Oh, right," I exclaimed. *Of course that's where they are.*

I led my drunken ducklings through the kitchen, out the back door, and down the cellar stairs once again.

When my eyes adjusted to the darkness, I saw that the three conspirators had set out a table with a jaunty red tablecloth. On it were displayed the silver *tastevins* that Renée had brought with their wide yellow-and-red neck ribbons artfully arranged. The table was decorated with a miniature traditional harvesting basket filled with freshly baked *gougères*, which I could smell from several feet away. I had heard about the legendary *gougères* from the *boulangerie* in Volnay many times. La Zette always declared they were "as big as your fist!" She had not been lying. Lucullus, our wedding caterer, had some stiff competition in the big *gougères* department, it appeared.

Renée held an accordion in her arms. "Laura, translate for me," she commanded.

She played a rollicking tune. "Hear ye! Hear ye!" she said, her voice easily loud enough to be heard over the music. "We have here before us six worthy Canadians who have proven they have Burgundian spirit. They have drunk copious amounts of our fine wine, eaten our delectable foods, and learned how to sing the *ban Bourguignon* with gusto. They have herewith earned the right to call themselves Honorary Burgundians! They hereby must swear to uphold the glory and honor of Burgundy wherever they travel in the world, and to remember that deep within each of them resides a Burgundian soul."

I did my best to keep up with the translations as Renée delivered her speech. My family looked slightly baffled, but suitably impressed.

"Lynda Bradbury, as the all-important matriarch of the Bradbury family," Renée intoned, "I am calling you up first." I ushered my mom up to the table. Renée gave another little squeeze of the accordion, and la Zette put one of the elaborate Burgundian necklaces around my mother's neck.

Renée leaned in and gave my mother a resounding kiss on each cheek. "Welcome to the sisterhood and brotherhood of Burgundy!" she declared. Then la Zette and Franck also kissed my mother, and Renée raised her hands in the unmistakable signal of a *ban Bourguignon*.

Then my mother was bidden to stand to the left of Renée in front of a wall of wine barrels lying on their sides. My family members were inducted one by one, and each induction merited a full rendition of the *ban Bourguignon*. I could see from the gleam in their eyes how pleased they were. My heart swelled at the sight of my Canadian family merging into my Burgundian family.

Afterwards, la Zette poured us each a celebratory glass of Burgundy *crémant* made in nearby Savigny-les-Beaune. Finally we all wandered outside and found ourselves in front of the low stone wall that ran alongside the village *salle des fêtes*, and which commanded a gorgeous view of the early evening sun casting its orange light over the vineyards below.

We posed for photos, happy and laughing. This was a moment of joy like Dr. Pradhan had been talking about in Nepal, I realized. I tried to freeze the moment and store it away in my heart, to remember in times when joy seemed like a distant continent.

The British woman emerged from Le Cellier Volnaysien. She cast us yet another disapproving stare and turned to walk up the road, presumably to the Aston Martin that was parked beside the church. With a gasp, I saw that she had tucked her demure skirt into her underwear and flesh colored stockings, giving us all full view of her stocking-covered bottom. I nudged my mother, who was standing beside me, and pointed.

"Now *there* is a satisfying sight," I said.

She looked in the direction of my finger and burst out laughing. I didn't think I had ever heard her laugh so hard. The woman stopped walking and turned her head to give us a scathing look, completely unaware of her skirt and nylon situation. My mother and I collapsed on the wall, clutching our stomachs in mirth. Everyone asked what was so funny, but we were laughing so hard we couldn't get the words out to explain. The muscles in my abdomen burned as if I had just done one hundred sit-ups. No matter the mess my life was in, I knew that I wanted Burgundy, and this feeling of fun and release, to be a part of it. Burgundy had a knack for releasing the joy and celebration in our souls that we hadn't even realized was clamoring to get out.

CHAPTER 15

That evening, after we had tucked in my family at the B&B, we got back to Franck's house just in time to catch Père Roux's phone call.

I could tell from the relief etched on Franck's features that he'd been given permission from the money-grabbing Père Gaillot to perform the ceremony.

When Franck hung up the phone, he came over and wrapped his arms around me in a solid hug.

"Now the only thing we need to do is find another church. The Père Roux suggested the one in Marey-les-Fussey. He performed a baptism there a few weeks ago and said it has recently been cleaned up. I'll make some calls, and hopefully we can go and check it out tomorrow.

I yawned. It had been an epic day, between our quick trip to Cluny and la Zette's legendary winetasting and inauguration. "I don't think you're going to have to rock me to sleep tonight," I said as we made our way up the crooked wooden stairs to Franck's tiny attic room at the top of the house.

Franck nipped the nape of my neck, making me yelp. "Maybe I'll want to," he said.

The next morning, I woke up to Franck shaking my shoulder. Bright sunshine poured in through the skylight, and I caught sight of a jet flying high overhead.

"I just got off the phone with the mayor of Marey-les-Fussey," he said. "He was delighted at the idea of having a wedding in their newly restored church. Let's go and have a look."

I was already throwing off the duvet. "Can we swing by the B&B to see if anyone in my family wants to come too?"

"Do you think they would?" Franck wondered. "I mean, it's just a church."

Even after all these years together, I was amused by how Franck could take the rich history of his home for granted, just as I had back in Canada with the endless forests and roaming orca whales. "It's a church that dates back to Roman times," I said. "Those may be a dime a dozen in Burgundy, but they're not in Canada."

A half hour later, we were in the courtyard of the B&B, where my family had just finished up one of Madame Dufrène's lavish French breakfasts of fresh croissants and *pain au chocolats*, homemade vineyard peach and *cassis* jams, bowls of fresh fruit with *crème fraiche* to dollop on top, and creamy *café au laits.*

"There's been a little change in plans," I explained. "It turns out we're not going to be married here in Magny-les-Villers after all."

"What do you mean?" My mother said.

"There was a mix-up with the priest and the churches," I said. Her eyes widened. "It's fine. Franck has already sorted it all out. We have to go and have a look at the church in Marey-les-Fussey though—just to confirm that it will work for us."

"But—" My mother began but couldn't seem to find any further words. It was true that these kind of things didn't happen as often in Canada as in France.

"Nothing to worry about," I said bracingly. "Go and get anything you need and we'll wait for you here at the car."

I could hear a lot of murmuring and expostulations inside the B&B, but when everyone came back out, they seemed to at least have decided not to ask any more questions for the moment. Sometimes there were advantages to being the bride that nobody wanted to stress out.

110

We piled everyone into the two cars, ours and my dad's, and Franck led the way to Marey. It only took about five minutes to get there—Villers-la-Faye and its surrounding villages were all situated very close together, or close enough to fit, as Mémé liked to put it, in a *mouchoir de poche*, or hanky.

Marey-les-Fussey was basically built on both sides of a small country road. On one side, the land and houses sloped down toward row upon row of vineyards. It was a smaller village than Villers—maybe one hundred and fifty people versus five hundred—but the church we saw as we pulled up was a picturesque little jewel.

Located near the far end of the village from Villers-la-Faye, just where the houses gave way to rolling fields of vineyards in every direction, it sat inside a beautiful wall of cream and ochre rocks, which appeared to have been recently cleaned. I knew from the wall's rambling structure that it was most likely built by the village stonemason several hundred years earlier. The church's exterior was gleaming with a recently applied coat of natural sand stucco. As I got out of the car, I could still smell the earthy scent of the mortar and lime the stonemasons had used. There wasn't a speck of dirt to mar the church's stunning ivory shade.

The church was so small it could almost be called a chapel. It was just one level, with one steeply peaked roof section for the bell. The stones framing the arched doorway were left uncovered, as were the stones surrounding a sweet, little stained glass window in the triangle of the roofline above the ancient wooden door. As my family and I explored the graveyard—which contained stone markers so old and weathered that the names of the deceased were no longer legible—Franck ran across the street to the mayor's office to grab the key. Without even going inside, I knew this church was perfect, and it was where Franck and I were going to be married.

Franck returned with a suitably impressive, rusted iron key about four inches long. He slid its intricate metalwork into its matching keyhole in the weathered wooden door.

Franck pushed the door open. It creaked in a most gratifying way. Something about the serene, hushed atmosphere inside made us all stop talking as soon as we crossed the threshold. To the right of the door stood a roughly hewn stone basin on a pedestal. It contained a few inches of holy water, and must have been carved by hand out of

Burgundy's famous marble. It had the trademark pink veins running through the rich, creamy rock.

Ten rows of wooden pews flanked the aisle, all scratched and old but polished to a high gleam. I moved down the aisle slowly, looking at my feet. The huge marble slabs were worn to a smooth surface through centuries of use, but still visible were the carvings in the stone, providing information about the people who had been interred underneath. The man I was standing on, whose last name was de la Charde if I was reading the old French correctly, had died in 1493. Below his name was an elaborate carving of a cross and the date of his death. To think I would be walking over the remains of Monsieur de la Charde from the late 1400s in two days in order to approach the altar and get married to Franck. I had never imagined I would have some guests from the Middle Ages at our wedding.

I was contemplating the wonder of this when a heavenly sound pierced the silence.

"Amazing Grace, how sweet the sound,
That saved a wretch like me…
I once was lost but now am found,
Was blind, but now, I see."

It was my older sister, Suzanne. Each note she sang reverberated in the sanctuary of this stone church. I was frozen by the beauty. Suzanne always had the most stunning voice, and I had asked her to sing this song—my favorite—during the wedding ceremony. I looked around me and saw that everyone was similarly spell-bound. Nobody moved an inch

"I once was lost, but now am found.
Was blind, but now I see…"

Nobody spoke. It was a moment of grace, where everything felt like it had fallen, magically, suddenly, into place and made sense. To speak would have shattered that.

Finally, Suzanne broke the silence. She cleared her throat. "Just testing the acoustics," she said, an apologetic tone in her voice.

We all rushed to thank her. I was born unable to carry a tune in a bucket, but if I had a voice like hers, I thought for the umpteenth time, I would sing all the time. Nobody would be able to stop me from singing.

We all explored the little church for a good quarter of an hour more, and none of us could find a single objectionable thing about it. On the contrary. It was perfect. Even more perfect than the church in Magny, perhaps. Had the stars aligned for Franck and me once again?

The next day my family, hosted by Franck's aunt Jacqueline and uncle Jean, spent the day at Jean's family house in Montigny. To be perfectly accurate, the house in Montigny was more of a small chateau than a house.

I was beginning to stress about all we had to do in order to get the cellars under the mayor's office in Nuits-Saint-Georges ready for our reception. Franck dismissed my concerns, telling me that it would all get done. "Jacqueline has asked one of her best friends from her nursing days to help us," he informed me. "Her name is Geneviève, and she is a master of efficiency. She and Mémé will have the cellars decorated in no time."

"Oh," I said. "Well…great. Have I ever met Geneviève?"

"No," Franck said, "but she's been invited to the wedding."

Compared to the cancelling priest and the change in church, inviting someone I didn't know to the wedding was really no problem at all. Especially if she was willing to help us. We could use all the efficiency we could get. Or so I thought.

My family's introduction to Montigny ran parallel with my own when I'd visited the first time as Franck's guest for Mémé's weekend-long eightieth birthday celebrations. They were stunned at the careless opulence of the chateau and its furnishings, and both thrilled and daunted by the sheer amount of food and drink served up by Jean, Jacqueline, and Mémé, who had also come along to help, along with Renée and Franck's parents.

They served themselves a piece of almost every type of cheese on the cheese platter and then found their eyes were bigger than their stomachs. After lunch, my aunt Sharon and my dad joined Renée for a catnap in the billards room—sitting straight up in their Louis XIV silk-upholstered chairs—while Jean and Franck played a game of pool on the luxurious wood and green-felted table in the middle of the room.

Jean of course brought out his famous bottle of cognac from the late 1800s, which had been hidden from the Nazis who had commandeered his family's chateau during the Occupation. He gave everyone a good taste in tiny, finely etched liqueur glasses, which had been handed down for generations.

All we were good for when we arrived back in Villers-la-Faye was bed. That left us with one more day to prepare for the wedding, I ruminated in the thirty second span between the time my head hit the pillow and when I fell asleep.

The next morning, we arrived bright and early at the cellar in Nuits-Saint-Georges to meet our troop of assistants—Jean, Jacqueline, Renée, *la cousine* Suzette, and the imposing Geneviève, who had the steely eyes and pinned-back bun that you would expect of a retired head nurse. I brought my own helpers—my aunt Sharon and my mother. Franck had gone with Suzanne, Greg, and Jayne to Beaune to take care of a number of errands there. That meant I was on my own for translation. However, one glance at Geneviève told me that it would be her, not me, leading the work party that day.

She seemed impatient throughout the customary introductions and *bises* and greetings, and cut them short to command that we all go downstairs. In the main reception room, the caterer's staff was assembling the round tables and chairs.

Geneviève commandeered one of these tables with a few curt words to the Lucullus staff. She took out a bunch of crafty-looking materials from the large leather bag she wore over her shoulder and ordered that my mother and Sharon sit down at the table and watch her.

Renée and la Zette, who were far more interested in eating and drinking than crafts as a rule, had already drifted off toward the kitchen, ostensibly to check that the Lucullus staff was doing everything *comme il faut*.

I watched, spell-bound, as Geneviève's agile fingers made quick work of the colored tissue paper, twist tie, and green felt for the stem, whipping up an admirable pale pink crepe-paper flower.

"Now!" she turned to me. "Tell your mother and aunt to start making them, just like I did. We will need quite a few so they mustn't dally."

I translated this to my mother and Sharon, who were looking more than a little intimidated by the task set before them. They cautiously picked up crepe paper and began to try to form it into petals as Geneviève had done. Luckily, Renée and la Zette called for Geneviève's help in the kitchen. As soon as she marched off my, mother and Sharon burst out laughing.

"What a dominatrix!" Sharon gasped. "I could almost picture her with a leather whip. Are you making yours right, Lynda?" she asked my mother.

My mother, generally a pretty crafty person, looked down at the mash of crepe between her fingers. "I don't think so."

"Well…fuck," Sharon said. "If *you* can't do it, there's no hope for me."

Geneviève chose that moment to come back. She took one look at her students' attempts at copying her flower and shook a stern finger at them. "*Non, non, non, non non!*" she said. "*Pas comme ça!*"

Somehow, I figured this didn't need translating.

Sharon and my mom were both looking at me with wide eyes, clearly signaling me to intervene. Luckily, at that very moment, Mémé called me from the far corner of the room. "Laura! I need you to give me your opinion in the kitchen!"

I raised my eyebrows at my mom and Sharon. "I'll just leave you to it then," I said with an apologetic shrug.

As I got up to leave, I tried not to look directly into their eyes, which telegraphed both an SOS call and shock at my betrayal.

Mémé kept me in the kitchen for quite a while, asking for my opinion about whether the French onion soup should be served with a slice of toasted, garlic- rubbed baguette on *top* of the soup or on the side. There seemed to be a difference of opinion with the catering staff about this matter and, according to Mémé, it was a questions of primordial importance. I voted for the "on top" option, of course, because that was what Mémé wanted. In my opinion, she had more than earned omnipotence in all culinary matters.

I planned on going back to checkin with the flower-makers in the cellar, but before I could finish with Mémé, Franck's best man, Olivier, burst into the kitchen.

"Franck needs you in Beaune," he said. "Something about the flowers. Your bouquet...or something. He sent me to get you because I drive faster than your brother-in-law." He seemed pleased by this fact.

He whisked me out and sped me to Beaune in record time, the vineyards and stone villagers alongside La Nationale whipping by us in a gold-and-green blur.

Franck was waiting for me in a café on the Place Carnot, where he was enjoying a cigarette and a coffee. After Olivier parked his Renault on the sidewalk—completely illegal but completely acceptable as far as he was concerned, apparently—Franck waved us in. "Come have a *café* first."

"We don't have time!" I protested.

"Things are...animated over in Nuits at the cellar," Olivier agreed with me. "I don't think we should delay in getting Laura back there."

I glanced over at him, thankful that he understood.

"Before I found you in the kitchen, I saw Geneviève berating your poor mother and aunt," he explained. "I'm not sure how long they're going to hold up."

"There's always time for a *café*," Franck insisted.

Olivier and I exchanged a glance. We both knew Franck too well. It would be quicker to just have the *café* than to stand there and argue with him about it.

We placed our order with the *garçon* who was quickly beside our table with his order pad in front of him.

"So, what exactly is this urgent issue with the flowers that requires my presence?" I asked.

"They can't get their hands on one of the types of flowers you agreed upon, so they want to know if it's acceptable to substitute another. "

"That's it?" I said. "Couldn't you have decided that without me?"

Franck looked askance at me. "I thought that sort of thing was of paramount importance for the bride. I didn't feel I could make the decision in your stead."

"Well, you could have," I grumbled. "If I find when I get back to Nuits that Sharon has murdered Geneviève with one of those big kitchen knives, it's on your head."

"That bad?" Franck said.

"That bad. I know she's an old family friend and everything," I said. "But does she have to be so astringent?"

"She's always been that way, but she does get a lot accomplished. She's helping us out of the goodness of her heart."

"Or because she misses bossing people around and yelling at them," I grumbled.

Olivier choked on his espresso. "It's true," he said apologetically to Franck.

I drained the rest of my espresso cup. "We've had our coffee. Let's go to the florist."

The florist was also on the Place Carnot, just a few doors down.

"What have you done with Suzanne, Greg, and Jayne?" I asked.

"Sent them to find wicker baskets for the baguette slices."

I nodded. That, at least, was not an unpleasant or impossible task.

Things at the florist should have taken five minutes—I merely had to approve the substitution of pale yellow roses for pale yellow lilies. However, this was Burgundy, and Franck and the florist were loath to let me go with so little conversation accomplished. To remedy this, the florist and my husband-to-be launched into a thorough (but entirely unnecessary) review of our the entire floral order for the wedding, all of the pick-up details, the state of the florist's wife's lumbago after she had visited an osteopath, and the florist's feud with the shopkeeper next door who sold all manner of wine-related paraphernalia for tourists.

"All made in China, I'd wager," concluded the florist darkly.

About two hours later, the florist finally let us go.

Olivier drove me back, perhaps even faster than the way there, while we commiserated about Franck's time dyslexia.

"We used to meet up and walk to the school bus stop together every morning," Olivier said. "We were late every day. It stressed me out so much that I developed eczema."

117

"Did the bus ever leave without you?" I asked, sympathizing completely.

"No. Franck somehow managed to charm the surly old bus driver. We always got yelled at, but he never left without us. If it was just me, he would have left," Olivier said.

"But if it was just you, you would never have been late," I said.

"True." Olivier smiled as we turned into the parking lot in front of la Mairie of Nuits-Saint-Georges.

It was with no small amount of trepidation that I went back into the main cellar. Sharon and my mother had their backs turned and were doing something to the stone wall on the opposite side of the room. They seemed to be muttering *sotto voce* between themselves. Geneviève sat at the table, her chair positioned so she could keep an eye on her serfs. She was making flowers with the efficiency of German bomb factories at the dawn of World War II.

"I'm back," I said, coming up behind her. "How is it going?"

She looked up at me down her long, thin nose. "They are incompetent." She waved a hand in the direction of my mother and aunt. "They cannot make a flower to save their lives. I will have to make them all myself, so I have given them the job of placing the flowers between the stones."

She stood up. "*Non! Non! Non!*" She marched forward and snatched the bunch of flowers from where Sharon has wedged them between two tight rocks in the cellar wall. "Not like that! *Franchement!*"

"I think we are going to take a little break, Laura," Sharon said to me, a mutinous gleam in her eye."

Geneviève must have understood a bit of English because she began to protest, but I interrupted. "Good idea. Come with me to the kitchen, and we'll see if we can find you something to eat."

We were barely out of the cellar when Sharon and my mother began pouring out their tales of abuse and exploitation at the hands of Geneviève. I found some cheese, baguette, paté, and *saucisson* for them, as well as a bottle of wine from Franck's uncle's domaine. Then I led them up the stairs where there was a rock wall where they could enjoy their break in the sunshine and as far away as possible from their oppressor.

I had planned to stay with them to soothe their spirits, but I had barely sat down when I was being called back down to the cellar by

Jean to give my opinion about the spacing of the chairs.

And so the afternoon went. Everyone wanted to know what I thought of this or that or the other thing, or wanted me to come and admire what they had accomplished. I could tell my mother and Sharon were growing more rebellious and desperate by the minute because of Genviève and her flowers, and probably would never forgive me for failing to rescue them from such indentured servitude.

Just when I thought my head was going to explode, I escaped up the cellar stairs for a breath of fresh air outside. I made the fatal mistake of standing up too soon and whacked my head on the huge slab of stone that topped the doorway.

I clutched my head and crumpled down to the stairs, where Olivier was sitting, meditatively smoking a cigarette.

Ça va, Laura?" he asked.

I needed no further prompting. I poured my frustrations out to him and concluded, finally, that this wedding business was more trouble than it was worth. Furthermore, my father had just informed me that rain was forecast for tomorrow.

Olivier patted me on the knee. "Tomorrow will be the best day of your life, Laura."

I snorted.

CHAPTER 16

Contrary to tradition, Franck and I slept together the night before our wedding. There were simply not enough beds, and besides, my nerves were jangling, so what I wanted more than anything was to feel Franck's warmth curled around me as I fell asleep.

I had somehow (I wasn't quite sure how) managed to keep my anxiety more or less at bay since my family had arrived. I was ever-conscious of it hovering around the edges of my mind, but being kept so busy had actually allowed me—temporarily I was well aware—to escape my thoughts. I was terrified about the possibility that my mind might catch up with me on my actual wedding day. That would be a complete disaster.

I woke up first and looked over at Franck, who was snoring gently with one hand flung up on his forehead.

This was the day.

After our fateful meeting in Nuits-Saint-Georges after my tap dance performance seven years before, Franck and I had fought—and managed—to stay together. We had braved the snows of Montreal during my undergraduate degree at McGill, we had sampled Parisian life during my exchange year at the Sorbonne, and we had even thrived in Nepal. The previous year at Oxford had been our hardest one yet as a couple. I always believed that on my wedding day I would feel like everything was all figured out—that I would no longer have any lingering questions or doubts about life.

I surveyed my mind for a few minutes. Nope. I was still uncertain about many things. I knew for certain that I loved Franck, but I had no idea where we were going as a couple, probably largely because I was so confused about my own direction. I didn't know if he would eventually get fed up with my anxiety and my ambition, and the fact that both these traits amplified in me when combined. I couldn't picture where we would be in two years' time. I was sure, though, that I would regret it if we didn't continue to fight to be together.

My heart was full of joy and worry and certainty and uncertainty all mixed together. It definitely wasn't the blissful mind of the fairy tale princess on her wedding day. Still, this was *our* wedding day, and at the end of it, I was at least guaranteed to have linked my future to Franck's in the most official way possible. And also to have eaten some truly delicious *piece montée*—if it made it across the street in Nuits-Saint-Georges in one piece, that was.

My friends Emmy and Melanie were arriving from Oxford by train that morning. At nine o'clock, Franck and I were going to pick them up. Then after that, Franck was going to drop me off at my parents B&B to get ready. My wedding dress, silk pumps, corset and stockings were already there.

I leaned over and gave Franck a gentle kiss. "Today's the day," I whispered in his ear.

He groaned and wrapped his arms around me. "That night didn't seem long enough."

"No regrets?" I asked. "No cold feet?"

He shook his head at me and smiled. "*Non.* But, *mon Dieu*, do I ever have a lot to get done today. I forgot that I have to be at the church at the same time as I need to be in Beaune to pick up the flowers. Also, before I fell asleep last night, I was thinking that if we don't find someone to translate the ceremony, all of your family and friends are not going to understand what is happening. And I'm not sure where to get the key to open the church in Marey, or what time exactly Père Roux is arriving and if he knows how to find Marey-les-Fussey—"

"The translation. *Merde.* Why haven't I considered that before now? Whom could we ask who is bilingual?"

"Emmy?" Franck suggested.

"It's sort of…last minute," I said. I imagined presenting her with the information as she got off a night train from London that she would be translating the entire church ceremony at five o'clock in the afternoon.

"She'll do it," Franck said, voicing an assurance that I didn't feel.

"About the flowers," I said, "Scott rented a fancy convertible. Maybe you could get him and Kathy to pick them up?"

"That's a great idea," Franck said. He gave me a kiss on the top of my head.

"Can you believe we made it this far?" I asked. "Nobody believed we would."

Franck pulled me in for a hug so tight that it was hard to take a deep breath. "I did," he whispered in my ear.

"We did it," I said and kissed his collarbone. He was crushing me against him so thoroughly that it was the only part of his body I could access.

"Not quite yet." He gave me one last, lingering kiss and then hopped out of bed. "First I have to figure out the flowers and the key and Père Roux."

Within forty minutes we had showered and eaten breakfast, and were waiting at the train station in Beaune to pick up Emmy and Melanie.

"Guess what!" Franck said to Emmy after she and Melanie had alighted on the platform and he had given them both the *bises*. "You have the honor of translating our wedding ceremony today."

"What?" said Emmy, blinking sleepily. "Surely you're joking."

"Uh. No," I said. "We just realized this morning that none of my family and friends will be able to understand a word of what is going on at the ceremony, so we thought we'd ask you if you wouldn't mind translating it for us. I know it's last minute and a huge favor to ask, but your French is so good and—"

"You mean I would be standing up in front of everyone and translating in real time? Today?" clarified Emmy, sounding horrified.

"Yes," Franck said, "that's exactly it."

"But—" she stuttered.

"*Merci!*" Franck said, and gave her another set of *bises*.

"Serves you right for being so annoyingly bilingual," said Melanie, an American doctoral student who specialized in Polish economics and hailed from Palo Alto.

We laughed and went and grabbed an espresso to wake them up, before dropping me off at the Communist B&B in Magny.

"But…what about the flowers?" I asked.

"I'll go see Scott next," Franck said.

"Shit! And picking up the *piece montée*!" Have we figured out a way to do that?"

A look of panic that didn't exactly give me peace of mind crossed Franck's features. "Maybe we could actually send someone over from the *vin d'honneur* to grab it," he said. That plan sounded rather vague. He gave me a quick kiss. "Don't worry. I'll figure it out."

"Is there anything I can do?"

"No. Just get ready. I'll send someone to drop off your flower hair thingy as soon as we pick up the flowers."

I had forgotten that the florist who was making my bouquet and all the flowers for the church had also made me a barrette for my hair with fresh flowers attached. "Are you sure?"

"I'm sure. Don't worry. It'll all be fine. Even if we forget stuff, nobody will notice. From now on, it's not about what we plan, but what we do with what happens."

With these dubious words of comfort, Franck sped off, sending a rooster tail of pea gravel in his wake. I stood in the courtyard, trying to make heads or tails of his last sentence. Either it was complete gibberish or profound beyond measure. I walked into the B&B, still unable to decide.

My family would be arriving any moment after their quick trip to the Beaune market that morning. I went into the front bedroom where my wedding dress hung on the curtain rod against the window. The dim light shone through it, highlighting the creamy, pearlish lustre of the raw silk.

Come to think of it, the sun looked considerably dimmer all of a sudden. I drew closer to the window and gingerly pushed the full crinoline skirt of my wedding dress aside so that I could see out.

After weeks of azure skies and sunshine, it had begun to rain. *Merde.*

CHAPTER 17

Three hours later, I was dressed in my corset and stockings, and the gazillion or so tiny little buttons that ran down my back were buttoned up. Suzanne had tonged my hair into loose curls, but my barrette made by the florist still hadn't been dropped off…I had begun to wonder if it ever would.

I had been short sighted in giving myself so much time to prepare for the wedding. I thought not feeling rushed would reduce stress. But on the contrary, I had too much time on my hands to entertain the prospect of suffering from a panic attack in the middle of the wedding ceremony. One of my worst triggers was being in a situation where it would be inappropriate to have a panic attack—as far as inappropriate situations went, my own wedding ceremony pretty much topped the list.

I tried to concentrate on the stiff silk that encased my torso and the scratch of the crinoline against my stockinged legs. I'd read somewhere that focusing on little physical details like that warded off the visual disturbances and hyperawareness that generally preceded an episode of anxiety.

I peered outside for the tenth time in about ten minutes. The rain was still coming down, harder now.

"Crap," I murmured.

"I'm sure it will clear up!" said my mother, jollying everyone along as she had been doing since we were small children. I squinted up at the dark gray clouds with doubt.

"Now, for your make-up," Suzanne announced.

"Ugh," I said, and plopped myself on the bed.

Make-up application was a skill that I had somehow neglected to learn. Suzanne was an expert at it, and could blend a foundation and apply three different colors of eye shadow so that they looked perfectly natural. Every time I tried to apply eye shadow, I invariably left myself looking like someone had sucker punched me. All I ever wore was mascara and, when I was feeling particularly fancy, tinted lip gloss.

"All right," I groaned.

"Hide your enthusiasm." Suzanne laughed.

Jayne came beside us to assist.

Suzanne came at me with a fingertip covered with foundation.

I recoiled from her touch. "Not too much."

"Close your eyes," she ordered.

"But—"

"Close your eyes!"

I closed them and tried to concentrate on the light touch on my cheeks and forehead and the feel of the brushes against my skin, and not think about whether I would recognize myself when I opened my eyes again.

"Does this make you remember your wedding?" I asked Suzanne.

"Sort of. I remember I hardly got a bit to eat all day and was almost keeling over by the time we left the reception."

"I don't think that will be a problem today," I said.

"Laura," Suzanne said, and I could tell from her voice that she was running out of patience, "you have to stop talking. This is precision work. I can't do this with your lips and face moving around."

Despite Suzanne's bossiness, being with my sister, back in our old dynamic, felt familiar. We hadn't been in the same city for any length of time since I had left for France on my exchange year, but it was comforting to know that no matter how much time we spent apart, our shared genetics and history made it effortless to pick up exactly where we had left off.

I nodded in agreement and tried to keep my mouth still as I felt Suzanne or Jayne (I wasn't really certain which) outline my lips with lip liner and fill them in with a tiny lip brush that tickled.

"Thanks for doing this," I said.

"Shut up!" Both Jayne and Suzanne said in unison.

"We'll never get it on if you don't stop talking," Jayne said.

I shut up…thinking that I was surprised Franck hadn't come by yet with my floral barrette and bouquet. I really needed to see him, before all the true craziness began. *Merde*. Had he forgotten about them? Given all that he had to do, that was not beyond the realm of possibility.

"OK, done," Suzanne said. "You can open your eyes now."

I followed her orders and stared in the aged mirror they had found in the bedroom and propped up against the windowsill across from where I was sitting.

My worries had been unfounded. I still looked like me, only prettier and far more photo ready.

"It's perfect," I said. "Thank you."

Suzanne consulted her watch. "Now we really need to get dressed."

"What should I do?" I wondered out loud.

My mom had come into the room at some point when my eyes were closed. "Stay where you are. Don't move. If you move you might get a rip or a stain or a smudge."

I wanted to protest, but she was right. It was a family joke how I could not seem to eat a meal without a good portion of it going down my top. "It's hard just…waiting," I said. I didn't mention my constant need to beat back the panic, but that compounded my dislike of sitting still with only my thoughts for company. My brain was not a particularly friendly place to hang out those days. It was more along the lines of a war zone.

Fifteen minutes went by, then twenty, then half an hour. I watched as everyone flew in and out of the bedroom, where I was perched on the bed, looking for a missing hairbrush or the right shade of eyeliner. I became more and more conscious of my heart, which didn't feel like it was beating normally. My aunt Sharon could only locate one of her formal shoes and had to unpack her entire suitcase to find the other, only to discover the culprit hiding under her bedside table.

Weddings were a lot of fuss, I concluded. And even though I wanted to get married, I was not a person who enjoyed fuss.

I asked my mom the time and did quick a calculation. My bouquet and my hair thing should have shown up over two hours previously. I began to fret again about Franck forgetting them. There wasn't even a phone in the bedroom. If I wanted to call him, I would have had to walk into the main house and disturb Monsieur and Madame Dufrène, who could have been in the middle of debating Trotsky-ism for all I knew.

The rain began to fall even harder. There was no way I could cross that courtyard and arrive on the other side un-smudged. I sat there, trapped in my finery, becoming more and more exasperated and agitated by my helplessness with every passing second.

Finally, I heard wheels crunch on the pea gravel. I hopped off the bed and ran to the window. It wasn't Franck's car—it was a convertible with the top incongruously down in the rain.

"Wha—?" I began.

I saw a familiar large form bound out of the car—my friend Scott, whom I had met in preschool and who had been my firm buddy ever since, had arrived with his fiancée, Kathy.

I wondered if I should go to the door to see what was going on, but I knew instinctively that I would face the wrath of my mother if I did so. Also, one of the glasses of wine that everyone was sipping from (I wasn't allowed one—too treacherous) would spill onto my dress *en route*. Murphy's law. I decided to stay where I was.

I tried to make out the animated conversation through the bedroom door but didn't have much luck other than catching a few ominous words. "Late. Little accident. Wet..."

Jayne came into the bedroom and shut the door behind her.

"What?" I asked, suspiciously. "Why did Scott come and not Franck?"

"Franck is...um...busy," she said evasively. "Anyway, Scott and Kathy brought your flowers, and Mom is just drying them out now."

"Why were they driving around in the rain with the top down?"

"The only instructions they can find are in Latvian, apparently. They can't figure out how to get it back up again."

"How wet are the flowers? Do they look OK?"

Jayne's eyes fixed on an apparently fascinating spot on the ceiling. "You know Mom. She can work wonders."

Uh oh. I sat on the bed, fretting. What was going on with Franck? Was he managing, or was he completely overwhelmed? I longed to see him so all of this somehow seemed more real.

A few minutes later, my mother came into the room with a round bouquet of lavender, yellow roses, blue delphiniums, and the occasional sprig of wheat. It was stunning in its simplicity. She also held a delicate barrette adorned with sprigs of wheat and lavender and trailing green things. My mother gingerly pulled out the pins holding my hairstyle in place and snapped the barrette in place.

She patted my head. "There you go. Lovely."

Our eyes met. A lump formed in my throat, and we both blinked back tears. I couldn't cry. Suzanne would kill me if I messed up my eye make-up now. My mom seemed to read my thoughts, because she winked at me and headed back to her bedroom to finish getting dressed.

A long, black car swung into the courtyard. Franck had told me it was a 1952 Citroën Traction Avant, a highly coveted collector's car. It was a spotless black with the Citroën "V"s in shiny silver on its tilted front. Out hopped the chauffeur—a friend of a friend of Franck's—in a proper black chauffeur's suit, including the matching hat.

I looked out at the pea gravel.

"This is going to be tricky," my mom observed. "Laura, do exactly as I say."

Under my mother's directions, Suzanne, Jayne, and my mother each lifted up a section of the skirt and directed me down each stair leading into the courtyard, as I couldn't see where I was going. I held my breath. Please don't let my legendary klutziness strike now. I had removed my glasses for the wedding and now was not only my usual uncoordinated self but also not able to see things properly. The whole undertaking struck me as so absurd that I hovered on the verge of laughter. It would be easier, I reflected, to strip down to my corset, and then put my dress back on in the car. Then again, there were all those tiny buttons...

My cream silk pumps were going to get muddy, but there was no way around that. Besides, I figured, my long skirt would cover them.

The chauffeur was holding the door open for me. *"Madame."* He folded his tall body into a bow.

"Bonjour," I said. "And *merci.* The car is just as beautiful as Franck said it was."

He nodded and smiled.

I slid gingerly across the cream leather seats. My sisters slid in beside me and my mother sat up front. My dad was going to drive my aunt and my brother-in-law, and follow us to Franck's house in Villers-la-Faye, which was the departure point for the procession through the village to the mayor's office for the civil ceremony.

The driver started the car, and the windshield wipers lazily wiped off the rain drops that splattered onto the windshield.

"Mariage pluvieux, mariage heureux." A rainy marriage is a happy marriage. *Do we have that saying in English?* I didn't think so.

I wasn't sure if this was a way to console couples who got rain on their wedding day, or whether the French truly believed in the saying that I had heard several times before. In any case, I agreed. *"Sûrement."*

The drive to Villers-la-Faye seemed to go far too fast. I wanted to slow this whole day down to a crawl.

We pulled in front of the green gate of Franck's house where a crowd of guests had already assembled. I could pick out my friends from England and Canada by their flamboyant, gorgeous hats. A cheer and a few stray *ban Bourguignons* rose from the crowd. My mother and sisters slid out of the car first so that they could hurry around and help me (and, more importantly, my dress). I slowly emerged, feeling like Cinderella—not because I felt astoundingly beautiful, but who else do you feel like when people are rushing around to hold up your skirts?

Mémé was by my side almost immediately. She ran up and gave me two firm kisses on each cheek, and then held me at arm's length with her rock iron grip. "Let me look at you," she said.

I met her eyes, but could feel myself blushing as she inspected me. If I had a fleck of mud on my cheek or a hair out of place, Mémé would see it.

"Parfait!" she declared after what seemed to me like a long wait. She gave me another set of kisses. "Just perfect."

I heard music. Accordion music that was getting louder. Where was it coming from? Then I remembered that Franck had found, through his web-like Burgundian connection, an accordion player named

Patrice to play for us throughout the day—it was hard to get more traditionally French than accordion music.

I caught a glimpse of the man who had to be Patrice making his way through the crowd, not stopping his playing for a second. My breath caught. He was straight out of central casting. Small Gallic stature, black pants, white shirt sleeves rolled up at the elbows, a black button-up vest, a red kerchief knotted around his neck, and a jaunty black hat. His beautiful accordion with "PIERMARIA" stenciled down its front was black, red, and white, as well. He even had a hooked nose, a mustache, a small beard, and a devilish look in his eyes. Patrice was like the distilled essence of France in one perfect package.

It took me at least fifteen minutes to kiss or hug everyone, depending on whether they were French or from Canada or Britain, all to the tune of Patrice's accordion. I kept scanning the crowd for Franck but couldn't see him.

Finally I made my way to the courtyard of Franck's family home, where he had kissed me hello on that nerve-wracking morning after we had gotten together at a local *discothèque* seven years earlier. Franck burst out of the kitchen door at that exact moment. We looked at each other, then shared a smile.

"Kiss! Kiss! Kiss!" the crowd began to shout. He strode toward me and gave me a kiss that was as unequivocal as that first one. Lip liner and lipstick be damned. The crowd cheered.

"Is everything OK?" I whispered to him.

"Fine," he answered, but with an air of distraction. "Just fine. Don't worry about anything. We need to pose for some photos."

We hadn't hired a professional photographer for the day, preferring instead to have the more casual shots taken by friends and family.

"I have to go get my parents and Emmanuel-Marie. I have no idea what they're still doing inside," Franck said.

He went inside the kitchen and re-emerged shortly after with his parents and nine-year-old brother, who was adorably dressed in shorts, a navy cardigan, red shoes, and a bow tie. We all posed in front of the huge, bright pink rhododendron that was planted in an old, wooden bread-rising trough from Mémé's decade as the village *boulangère* across the street. Thankfully the rain had paused for the photos, but the clouds above still looked gray and engorged.

I had never seen Michèle, Franck's mother, look so lovely. Her short hair was styled into a flattering pixie cut, and she wore a chic, white embroidered suit. She was smiling and radiant.

Come to think of it, my family looked pretty smiling and radiant as well.

"You look beautiful," Franck leaned over and whispered to me between photos.

I glanced down the bodice of my dress. "You think we made a good choice?"

"Yes. I'm also looking forward to seeing what you're wearing underneath."

I smiled with satisfaction knowing I'd kept that, at least, a surprise.

I squeezed Franck's hand and posed with him for all the people snapping photos. Franck was wearing a dark olive suit that we had chosen for him in Oxford and a pale yellow tie flecked with the tiniest pale blue dots that complemented the pale yellow flowers in my bouquet. "How are all the things…you know…*going?*"

"Fine," he said blithely. But I could tell from the coiled energy in his fingers as we held hands that he was running on adrenaline, and that his head was surely filled with the hundred things he had to do and manage between now and the reception.

"The accordion player?" I said. "He is absolutely *perfect.*"

"Patrice? I know!" Franck said, a momentary triumphant light in his eye. "Renée said he is a superlative player as well, and she knows her accordion music."

"Let me know if I can do anything," I said. "I want to help."

"But this is your day," he said.

"This is *our* day."

He looked at me, then leaned over for a kiss. Out of the corner of my eye, I could see the brilliance of at least twenty flashes going off at once.

We were going to get married. No hitches would matter after this point. Or so I thought.

CHAPTER 18

After the photo shoot, it began to sprinkle rain again, so Franck organized us to begin the procession from his front gates. Patrice led the way with his accordion, of course. My father and I came next, with Franck's tall uncle Jacques, Renée's oldest son, holding his umbrella over me. Then came my sisters and my brother-in-law, Franck's parents, and then... well, I couldn't see any further back in the line, but it seemed to me like we made quite an impressive parade.

Patrice began a new song on his accordion—quite a jaunty, celebratory tune—and we started walking up the hill past Mémé's old *boulangerie*.

We turned left in front of the church where Franck's parents had gotten married and Franck had served as an altar boy. It was shame that the village priest, Le Père Bard, had stopped performing marriages because of his advanced age. Still, Père Roux had definitely grown on me, and in the end was highly preferable to the dastardly Père Gaillot.

I was surprised, and a bit awed, to see villagers gathered on either side of the road despite the rain. They clapped as we walked slowly by, and many shouted "*Vive la mariée!*" Long live the bride!

Out of the corner of my eye I could see that many of them joined in our procession as we went by, clearly not caring that they were dressed in their faded *bleus de travail* or ratty old flowered housecoats. As a rule, French civil ceremonies were always open to the public. My opinion was, the more the merrier.

We neared the mayor's office, quintessentially French with its *bleu, blanc, et rouge* flags out front, a bright yellow La Poste mailbox mounted by the front door, and a *tilleul* tree growing outside. Would I remember all my lines correctly? Where was Franck? I glanced behind me but couldn't see him in the crowd of people. He had just been behind me. Where had he gone?

The mayor was standing on the front steps of Villers-la-Faye's mayor's office. He was actually filling in for the regular mayor, a village woman who had grown up with Michèle and who was, like most good French citizens, enjoying her five weeks of annual vacation somewhere on the French Mediterranean.

He, like Patrice, looked the part. He was slight and small in that Gallic way, and had a prominent nose, jet-black hair, and equally black eyes. He wore a tricolor sash over his dapper camel-colored suit and tie. After spotting me immediately, he grasped my shoulders, drawing me in for a smacking *bises*.

"That," he said before releasing me, "is the privilege of monsieur le maire, and one that I plan to take full advantage of. *Félicitations*," he added, scanning the crowd. "And where is your husband-to-be?"

I turned and scanned the crowd, and my heart did a strange little thump when I couldn't find Franck. "He must be back there somewhere," I said, feigning a confidence that I did not entirely feel.

"He will surely be here soon with a beautiful bride like you waiting!" The mayor studied the crowd and drew his eyebrows together. "I'm not certain we are all going to fit," he said. "Some people may have to stand in the hallway or outside."

I didn't see any solution to that, so I just shrugged. Where *was* Franck? He had always been better than me at crowd control. I noticed some villagers who had not been invited jostling their way to the front with a typical French disregard for queues. The Canadian and British guests looked shocked, but were too polite to say or do anything. I beckoned my family, and anyone else who I knew had been invited to the wedding, up front near me.

"*Venez!* Come!" The mayor beckoned me to the front of the room with his hand. "I'll show you where to stand." He led me in front of an antique wooden desk, which had a large photo portrait of Jacques Chirac, the French president, mounted behind it. I had to admit Chirac looked extremely presidential in the photo—although I had always preferred François Mitterand.

The crowd surged in behind us. As they moved up to stand beside me, I spotted my witnesses, Alana and Franck's sister, Stéphanie who, after all, had been the reason we had met. I also spotted Franck's witnesses—his friends Olivier and Nicholas. Mémé, was gliding to the front of the crowd on Uncle Jean's arm like Moses parting the Red Sea.

"Where is Franck?" I whispered to Olivier. He scanned the crowd and his eyes widened.

He shrugged. "I have no idea. You know how he is…always late."

Surely he would be coming? The idea that he might *not* be coming triggered the possibility that I had been dreading for days—a panic attack during my actual wedding. My heart pounded. Too fast, surely. Far too fast. Everything around me receded into a warped and menacing unreality, as if I were stuck inside of a Hieronymus Bosch painting.

I made the mistake of turning my head slightly to look over my shoulder for Franck. No Franck, but countless pairs of eyes fixed on me…waiting… My neck and face began to burn, and I couldn't seem to breathe without making a conscious effort to do so. I couldn't get in any air. Where *was* he? *Oh my God.* I was in the middle of my worst nightmare.

The conversation died down and silence blanketed the room. It was so quiet I could hear the tick of the antique clock mounted on the far wall.

Blotches of black floated across my line of vision. I tried to blink them away.

Tick. Tick. Tick.

I knew—just instinctively *sensed*—when everyone started to have the same thought as mine. *Has Franck changed his mind?*

Somebody let out a nervous titter.

Tick. Tick. Tick.

The floor began to sway under my feet. *I am going to pass out right here. I am going to pass out in front of all these people.*

Tick.

My adrenaline took on an edge of anger. *How could Franck do this to me? Abandon me here, alone, in the center of this crowd?*

Tick.

My bouquet shook in my hand. It took every ounce of concentration not to just let myself keel over.

135

Tick. Tick. I couldn't bear one more second of the silence.

"Well," I said, in a shaky voice, "this has been fun."

The crowd roared with laughter, and the tension broke for a moment. If Franck didn't show up though, I knew it would resume worse than before.

A clammy sweat began to bead on the back of my neck.

Tick.

Tick.

Tick.

Just then I heard a murmur in the back of the crowd. Anything was better than that silence descending over the room again.

Franck burst through. He was breathing hard as though he had been running.

"*Enfin!*" I said. Finally! Even the Anglophone guests picked up on my meaning and laughed.

"What the hell happened?" I asked before the hilarity died down. "Everyone thought you had decided not to come."

He looked at me. "Even you?"

"I had begun to wonder."

"I'll tell you later," he said. "It wasn't my fault."

According to Franck, it was never his fault when he was (always) late. This time, though, I noticed that André, who I now realized had also been missing, had taken his position in the front of the crowd beside Michèle. He looked as harried as his son. What had they been doing? He didn't have to *chase* after Franck, did he? My palm itched to smack my husband-to-be. My panic had subsided, but it had been replaced by an unsettling combination of relief, confusion, and rage.

Franck had shown no doubts leading up to then, not even that morning, but when it got down to the wire, weddings did strange things to people.

"Are we ready?" The mayor said, raising one single, questioning eyebrow at the two of us.

I didn't know how to answer this. *Are we?*

"Completely," Franck said. His voice conveyed such assurance and confidence that all of my crazy emotions that had been pinging off each other began to settle.

"*Oui,*" I said. I planned to ask him what happened when it was just the two of us again. I surveyed the crowd. That would have to wait.

The idea of a civil ceremony before the church ceremony was brilliant, I realized as we made our way out of la Mairie, now officially husband and wife, with our brand new laminated *livret de famille* to prove it.

All the stress of actually getting married was behind us now. We had done it in the remarkably expedient and pragmatic civil ceremony that had remained pretty much unchanged since shortly after the French revolution. It involved, as far as I could tell, a lot of showing one's ID papers and signing and stamping documents. Despite France being the country of romance, those revolutionaries didn't waste any time on sentimentality. Before I knew it, Franck was giving me a kiss, and we were husband and wife in the eyes of *la République.* Jacques Chirac smiled his approval from the wall.

We posed for even more photos in front of the mayor's office in under the spitting rain. Emmanuel-Marie came over to give me a hug, and I could hardly believe that this little brother with his red Buster Brown-style shoes and navy bow tie was now, officially, my brother-in-law.

Franck pulled me into the backseat of the Citroën. Jacqueline pressed a full glass of *mousseux* each into our hands and settled the silver champagne cooler beside Franck.

The driver honked and honked as the car purred off in the direction of Marey-les-Fussey for our church wedding.

"Could you take the long route, please," Franck said, "so that everyone else has time to get there?"

The chauffeur nodded, ever discreet. Franck's shoulders dropped, and he settled back against the seat, looking grateful for the chance to rest for a few minutes.

I leaned over and kissed him. "Hello, husband."

He kissed me back. "Hello, wife."

We both grinned. We had done it.

"What happened? Where did you disappear to?" I asked.

"I forgot that we needed to pay the mayor for the ceremony, so I ran back home with my dad to scrounge up one hundred francs. It took us a while."

I punched his shoulder. "It was awful. Everybody was staring at me and wondering if you had changed your mind."

"Who would think that?" Franck asked, as if truly bewildered.

"That is usually what people tend to think when the groom fails to show up for the wedding.

"I *did* show up."

"Yes, but for ten minutes there nobody knew that you would."

"I'm sorry," he said, "I had no idea. I just knew I had to pay the mayor. I figured you couldn't start without me, so…"

"So everyone could just wait? Including me? I swear to God, Franck Germain, it would have served you right if I had decided to marry the mayor himself. He was quite dapper."

Franck laughed and sipped on his *mousseux*.

"It feels surreal, doesn't it?" I said.

Franck nodded.

Looking out the window, I could see the car was ambling through the vineyards in the direction of Savigny-les-Beaune. I thought about my first few weeks in Burgundy, as well as those first few weeks after I met Franck. Part of me felt amazed to find myself there, married to Franck seven years later. Yet part of me also felt that destiny had a strong hand in bringing us together and keeping us together.

"I almost passed out, you know," I said, conversationally.

"What?" he demanded. "When?"

"At la Mairie. I was all by myself up there in the front. Everybody was staring at me and wondering…then I started wondering…then I got panicky."

"Was it bad panicky?" Franck asked.

"Yes. I truly think that if you hadn't arrived when you did, I would have fainted in front of everyone. I was starting to hyperventilate."

"But you shouldn't have worried." Franck squeezed my hand. "You know I would never abandon you."

"Deep down I know that," I said, staring down at my lovely bouquet. "But everyone was staring at me. It was the worst possible place to have a panic attack so, of course, that's what happened. This anxiety thing, it's not reasonable. It's even a little bit crazy. *I'm* a little bit crazy. Do you realize what you've gotten yourself into?"

Franck reached over and slid the bouquet out of my hands, resting it gently on the seat beside me, pulling me closer to him.

"I like that you're not perfect," he said. "I feel bad for you about your anxiety because I know how it makes you suffer, but it's one of the things that makes you human. It makes you *Laura*, you know?"

I rubbed my forehead. "I'm a mess."

"I know," he said. "But what about me? I'm never on time for anything. I talk too much and don't listen nearly enough—"

"Like every other French person on the planet."

"Still…I don't do nearly as well in day-to-day life as I do in crisis situations. I never check the time… We're both imperfect, and the fact that we've just gotten married means not only do we accept that in each other but we also *love* that in each other."

CHAPTER 19

By the time our Citroën pulled in front of the stone church of Marey-les-Fussey, my anxiety had vanished and I was in a celebratory mood. It was amazing how everything seemed more joyous when I let go of my expectations and all the things I thought I should be and the way things should unfold.

Our driver had done a good job taking the longest route possible to Marey, because it looked as though everyone else had arrived and most people had already gone inside the church.

My dad was waiting for me by the door of the church, but by the time Franck and I got to the door, the music we had chosen to walk down the aisle to, Andrea Bocelli's *"Con Te Partiro,"* was already playing—too early. We had given Martial the job to start the music, but he must have misunderstood the timing. Either that or he was too eager to get to the end of the religious ceremony and start ringing the church bells. I had hardly any time to get emotional because we hurried into the church in a strange sort of huddle. First Franck on his mother's arm. Then me on my father's.

As I walked down the aisle, I smiled back at everyone who smiled at us. I caught the eye of Monsieur Lacanche, who must have gotten there early as he and his wife had prime spots. He gave me a nod and what looked like a sincere smile. Maybe I had misjudged him too? Or maybe I was just in a particularly magnanimous mood.

My eyes welled up with tears as I looked upon all the familiar and beloved faces in the crowd. That was the first time I'd experienced such an overlap of my lives in Canada, Oxford, and Burgundy—as if separate universes were finally converging.

After my father left me by Franck's side in front of the altar—and in front of a majestic Père Roux, who was resplendent in a white cassock with an orange-and-yellow sash thing around his neck—I admired Franck's choice of church. The newly cleaned stonework of the curved ceilings glowed a rich cream color. Jewel-toned beams of light shone through the stained glass windows, landing on the polished wooden benches and the carved flagstones on the church floor.

When the Bocelli song stopped, Père Roux's voice boomed out over the congregation, welcoming everyone on this joyous occasion. He explained that our friend Emmeline was going to translate the ceremony. He certainly possessed a commanding presence in the front of the church that was at complete odds with his everyman demeanor in the café in Cluny. Emmy stood, her straw hat perched stylishly on her blond curls, and began to translate in her plummy British accent.

The ceremony sped by. Both Franck and I said, "*oui, je le veux*" when we were supposed to, and at the end when we were allowed to kiss, melted into one another with relief.

We signed the church registry at the front with our parents and our witnesses, and Franck, and I were left alone with the Père Roux for a moment while everyone was filing outside.

"*Merci, mon Père,*" I said.

"*De rien,*" he said. "You just have to promise that you will invite me to officiate at the baptisms of your children." He laughed.

I thought back to that piece of paper I had signed for Father Strawbridge. I definitely wasn't ready yet, but I did feel one step closer to wanting children. "It's a deal," I said.

Martial sneaked back into the church and looked a bit taken aback when he saw our priest still there. "I'm a bell ringer," he explained to Père Roux. "I was just going to ring the bells for Franck and Laura. It's actually my day job. I have a key." He brandished a huge, ancient iron key.

"Be my guest." Père Roux swept one of his robed arms toward a little door to the left of the altar. Martial disappeared, and before I knew what was happening, the bells began to peal overhead. I didn't think I'd ever heard church bells so loud. Martial clearly intended to give us a proper send-off.

Franck hooked my arm. "I think that's our cue, *ma femme*."

That was right. I was his wife. We were now officially married, by both a mayor and a priest. We had tied the knot tight.

I had barely put one cream silk pump-shod foot outside the church when I felt something like little bee stings all over my face. I squeezed my eyes shut and took a step backwards into the church again.

"What the hell was that?" I asked Franck.

"Rice," Franck said. "They're throwing it at us.

Huh. I knew it was tradition to pelt newlyweds with rice, but no one had ever told me it hurt so much. Somebody out there had an impressive arm on them. We ventured out again to see Franck's little half nieces and nephews, under the encouragement of la Zette, eagerly throwing fistfuls of the stuff at us.

We posed for a bunch of photos, smiles of relief on both of our faces. We had done it.

The bells were still thundering overhead when we climbed back into the Citroën. Villagers had started to arrive outside the church, no doubt curious about all the commotion. The church bells surely had not rung that triumphantly since the end of the Second World War.

Our driver shut the car door behind us. "To Nuits-Saint-Georges?" He had gotten in and turned around to face us.

"Yes, but again we should be the last to arrive," Franck said. "I know where we should go."

"Where?" I asked.

"Can you take us to Pernand-Vergelesses?" Franck asked the driver. "Do you know the Virgin Mary statue on the hill above the village?"

"Of course," he said, and turned around and started the ignition.

I nestled against Franck's side as the car pulled away from the front of the church. As we waved at all our friends and family outside, the driver honked several times. Every time we passed a car on the road, the other driver honked his congratulations and our driver honked back.

I laced my fingers with Franck's, thinking about all we had been through together that had led us to this point.

"No regrets?" Franck said, arching an eyebrow at me.

I squeezed his hands. "I'm not sure about a lot of things," I said, "but I'm sure about this."

Soon we were circling up the road to the Virgin Mary statue above

Pernand-Vergelesses, where Franck had taken me the first afternoon after we had met. I thought back to that day, how I had been so worried that he would pretend as though we hadn't gotten together the night before. And then, when that didn't happen, that he was some kind of lunatic who was going to kidnap me and have his way with me. That didn't happen either, of course.

The driver said he was going to stay near the car and have a cigarette, which was very discreet of him. Franck and I walked across the field in the spitting rain toward the statue. Luckily, the weather must have scared away any potential picnickers so we had the entire place to ourselves.

We walked to the Virgin Mary, holding hands. I looked up into her serene face.

"*Merci*," I said to her.

"That wasn't me you were thanking, was it?" Franck asked.

"*Non*," I said, "I was thanking her. I don't know why, but I suspect she had something to do with us…with all of this."

Franck was still looking up. "*Moi aussi*," he agreed.

I would have sat down on the base of the statue, as I had with Franck when he had first brought me up there, but the stone was dark with water from the rain, and I was wearing an ivory wedding dress.

We turned to the view of the valley, which usually stretched out as far as the eye could see—first vineyards, then the flat plains, and then, on a clear day, the bumpy distant outline of the Alps.

That day, though, because of the weather, all we could see were a few rows of vineyards down in the valley and the church steeple of Pernand-Vergelesses peeping out of the mist. It was an apt metaphor for my current vantage point in life. I couldn't see beyond going back to Oxford in September, slogging through another year of law classes and trying to manage my anxiety. Everything beyond that was unclear. But Franck was beside me, his arm wrapped firmly around my shoulders. That made my lack of vision seem less scary somehow. I felt sure of *him*, and that was enough. As for the rest…I would figure it out. *We* would figure it out.

I let my head fall to the crook of his shoulder. "I wonder what's next for us," I murmured.

"I don't know," Franck murmured. "Lots of adventures."

"Are you sure you don't regret not marrying a nice Burgundian girl from one of the villages around here?" I asked. "Things would be simpler."

"Did I ever ask for simple?" Franck said, pulling me closer.

"No," I said. "Thank God for that, or rather, thank *la Vierge* of Pernand."

"You were the first girl I brought here, did you know that?"

"The only?" I said, a bit surprised in spite of myself.

"The only," Franck said, and sealed it with a kiss.

CHAPTER 20

By the time we got to Nuits-Saint-Georges, we could see from all the cars parked in the haphazard French way outside the stone building of the mayor's office that, as they had at the church in Marey, pretty much everyone had arrived before us. Could the *vin d'honneur*—the traditional drinks that heralded the beginning of the wedding reception in France—start without the bride and groom, I wondered? Of course *kir*, served with local *mousseux*, would be the drink of choice. I was eager to get my hands on a glass of one.

Franck led me down the narrow, steep stone stairs into the seemingly endless cellars under the mayor's office. I had forgotten to ask Franck how old these cellars were, but like most cellars in Burgundy, they probably had been around in some form or another since Roman times, with just the buildings on top changing throughout the centuries.

We could hear the noise of French and English chatter and the rousing tune of Patrice's accordion. When we entered the room— where the *vin d'honneur* was set up on a long table with row upon row of glasses and bottles—the entire crowd burst into a raucous *ban Bourguignon*. Patrice nimbly changed from his previous tune to accompany them. A glass of *kir royale* was pressed into my hand and one into Franck's. We were urged to drink, and after our first sip, the crowd broke into a second *ban Bourguignon*. I looked around and saw that everybody held a glass and that most of my Canadian and British friends already sported rosy cheeks and a shine in their eyes that only *kir* could impart.

The *vin d'honneur* finally wound down. After we had spent a good hour or so drinking and toasting and doing impromptu dances and chatting, we were ushered into an adjacent cellar—this one much larger, with the set tables and all of the paper flowers decorating the walls, thanks to the bossy Geneviève, and my mother and Sharon, her mutinous helpers.

I seemed to be pushed along by the tide of people. Instead of having a "high table," Franck and I had decided that we would just sit at another round table with our witnesses from the ceremony and siblings. I was relieved to see a woman setting up the *piece montée* in the far corner of the room, as this meant that it must have made its way across the street intact. I'd have to remember to ask Franck how exactly he had pulled off that miracle.

Inside the wine cellar, it was hard to tell the time, but I estimated that it had to be around eight o'clock in the evening at least.

We hadn't been seated for long when white-aproned serving staff began pouring out of the kitchen area and putting a piping hot dish of twelve *escargots de Bourgogne* in their shells in front of each person. I sighed in anticipation.

I picked up my pinchers and seized a snail shell, then plucked out the little garlicky, parsley-infused beast inside with my small fork. I popped it into my mouth. *So good.* Buttery, herby, garlicky, snaily deliciousness—how had I lived for seventeen years without eating snails? I felt, as I always did when eating *escargots* in Burgundy, that I had to make up for lost time.

I felt a hand on my shoulder. Monsieur Beaupre was at my side. "Do you remember, Laura?" he asked. "We were the first ones to introduce you to *escargots?*"

"Of course I remember!" I said. "That wonderful meal at la Maison des Hautes-Côtes." I remembered being so worried about having to eat snails, and then so shocked when I realized I actually loved them. I reached up and squeezed his hand. "I'm so glad you were my first host family."

"I am glad too," Monsieur Beaupre said. "It is a beautiful wedding." He squeezed my shoulder again. "I'd better go back to my table before—*mon Dieu*—my *escargots* get cold!"

I turned back to mine to see that Franck had refilled my glass with red wine from the Luberon supplied by his uncle who owned a winemaking domaine in Provence. Even though it wasn't a Burgundian wine, Jean-Marie—Franck's uncle and godfather—had been trained as a winemaker in Beaune, so his wine had an undeniable force and a Burgundian style that did an admirable job standing up to the snails.

After we had all mopped up every last drop of escargot sauce with slices of fresh baguette, the ever-efficient serving staff swooped in and removed the ceramic plates. Minutes later, they replaced them with plates heaped with fragrant *boeuf Bourguignon* and crispy, creamy *gratin dauphinois*. Each table was also supplied with three traditional ceramic pots of Dijon mustard with tiny wooden spoons inside.

The *boeuf Bourguignon* smelled just as good as the batch that had been simmering away in the attached industrial kitchen at Lucullus when we were there planning the meal. The sauce was a heady mixture of red wine, butter, onions, thyme, laurel and bay leaf. It shimmered in the dim light, silkily coating the stewed chucks of local charolais beef.

I inhaled appreciatively. "Hmmmmmmmmmmmmm."

"And Father Strawbridge believes food has nothing to do with God," Franck scoffed. "Clearly, he has never had the privilege of eating in Burgundy."

The waiters came around and served us large glasses of Gevrey-Chambertin wine, which we had chosen to accompany the main course. I took a small sip. Powerful. Earthy. A perfect accompaniment to the *boeuf*.

The mustard pot was being passed around and I put a generous dollop on my plate.

The clatter of cutlery against china signaled that everybody had been served and was diving in.

The layers of paper-thin sliced potatoes, moist with garlic-infused cream and sprinkled with emmenthal, soaked up the sauce of the *boeuf* and melted in my mouth. The meat was so tender from hours of braising that it fell apart when I was trying to fork it into my mouth. A few droplets of the sauce splashed onto the front of my dress. *Oh well.* The light was dim.

"No one's going to be complaining about the food," I whispered to Franck. "I don't think even Mémé or Renée will be able to find anything to criticize." That was saying something.

"Do you think all of our foreigners like it?" Franck asked.

It took me a second to realize that by "foreigners" he meant my fellow Canucks and our British friends. I looked over to the table where Emmeline and Melanie sat with a bunch of my Canadian friends. They were all eating and laughing and cleaning their plates and emptying their glasses with alacrity. "Looks that way," I said. "Besides, who would be crazy enough not to like *boeuf Bourguignon?*"

"Certainly not *our* friends," Franck said.

"Exactly."

After a while, the servers returned with huge terra-cotta dishes filled with food and served seconds to anyone who wanted it. Many did, but I declined. I knew we had the cheese course coming next.

I did, however, enjoy a second glass of the Gevrey, which put me in a contemplative mood.

I felt like things with the Beaupres had gone full circle. Of course we would never again be as close as we had been when I was a young, non-French-speaking, seventeen-year-old girl arriving in Burgundy for the first time. Still, I would be forever grateful for their kindness and love at such a pivotal time, and I hoped that they cherished those memories as much as I did. I believed perhaps the Beaupres now understood why I had to choose Franck over the Ursus Club, and hoped they had forgiven me.

It was even possible the Lacanches were thawing slightly toward Franck and me. Franck had been right to invite them to the *vin d'honneur.* They could think what they wanted, so there was no reason not to be civil.

"Is everything all right?" Franck clinked his glass lightly with mine, which I held close to my chest—probably not such a brilliant idea given the almost still-pristine wedding dress I wore.

"Yes. Everything is perfect—just as Olivier promised me it would be."

"Olivier?"

"Yes. When I was freaking out a bit yesterday he assured me that today would be perfect—the best day of my life, in fact."

Franck burst out laughing.

"What?" I asked.

"He told me the exact same thing when I was stressing out yesterday."

We chuckled. "So," I asked, "do you think he was right?"

Franck smiled at me over the rim of his glass. "Yes I do."

The servers came out of the kitchen again, bearing trays with little glass cups, each one filled with pear sorbet and drenched with Poire Williams.

"I had completely forgotten about the *trou Normand*," I said to no one in particular.

My little sister Jayne got my attention from across the table. "What is this?" She pointed at the glass that had just been set in front of her.

"It's a *trou Normand*," I said. "It's supposedly to help everyone digest before the cheese course."

"Not supposedly!" said Franck's friend Nicolas, who had acted as one of Franck's witnesses. He had clearly picked up on what I had said in English. "It works. Every French person knows that. It's science."

"Oh really?" I said. "Science?"

"Absolutely," Nicolas answered.

"If you say so," I said to Nicolas in French, and then switched to English to warn Jayne. "Brace yourself. The alcohol is strong enough to curl your hair."

I watched, amused, as Jayne took a spoonful. She coughed and turned bright red. "It's good," she gasped. "Really good."

I took a spoonful of mine, and had to suppress a cough myself. They certainly hadn't stinted on the Pear Williams. The icy sorbet itself, though—cold with a light fruity flavor—did slide down my throat very well after the richness of the first two courses.

Some time later, after the *trou Normand* had been consumed and cleared, a *ban Bourguignon* began to ripple through the room, led first by Patrice and his jaunty accordion music, and then by Renée, who had also brought her accordion. I caught sight of Renée's daughter, Hélène, who also played the accordion and had brought along her instrument—in her case a smaller version.

I sat up straighter to try and see what was going on. The accordion trio, it seemed, had provided the requisite fanfare for the huge wooden platters of cheese being carried into the room by the servers.

I had been right to save room for the cheese—a large wedge of creamy Citeaux, made by the monks in the first Cistercian monastery just up the road from Nuits-Saint-Georges, a slice of the pungent l'Ami du Chambertin, a knifeful of the oozing Époisses…

André instructed the servers to serve everyone from the

151

nabuchodonosor of Grand Échezeaux that had been given to Franck on his communion, and which his parents had saved for his wedding day. The bottle was massive and contained fifteen litres of wine, so it went a surprisingly long way.

I thought back to photos I had seen of little Franck with his hair cut in a bowl cut. He was wearing white altar boy robes and a massive wooden crucifix around his neck. When I was in my classes in high school, longing for someone to fall in love with, who would have thought that I would have to travel to France to find him? And that even after travelling to France, fate would be clever enough to put him in my path? Something about how all that had happened was still mysterious and magical.

The Échezeaux was also downright magical, standing up to two rounds of servings without oxidizing, a common problem with the large bottles of aged wines. It was a deep rust with garnet overtones and had an earthy, succulent bouquet. There were few wines that our cheese selection wouldn't overpower. This was one of them.

Guests began streaming by our table to give their good wishes and press envelopes in Franck's hands—André's parents from Beaune; Geneviève, the *decorateur-generale*; the Lobreaus from Savigny, some of my favorite winemakers who also gifted us with four *rehoboams* (wine bottles about six times the size of average bottles) of Savigny-les-Beaune Premier Cru.

"For the baptisms!" Pierre slapped Franck on the back.

"We'd better get to work!" Franck said. When he winked at me, I had a moment of fear. I still wasn't ready...or at least I didn't think I was. I had to figure out all of this law stuff and where we were going to live and...

Maybe I wasn't quite ready for children, but I did feel *readier* maybe than I had that day back in Oxford. That was something, wasn't it?

Before I knew it Franck and I were being summoned to the side of the room where the *pièce montée* had been set up in all its wobbly glory.

I was given a knife, but I wasn't exactly sure what to do with it. How was I supposed to cut a precarious tower constructed of cream puffs and spun caramel?

Franck gently took the knife I held in my hand as we posed for the obligatory photos, and handed me a long fork, a silver spatula, and a plate.

I studied the tower, not at all sure of the best way to proceed. Maybe this was one of those things like showering in a bathtub with only a shower attachment hooked up to the tap—you had to be French to know how to do it.

"Are you sure you trust me to do this?" I whispered to him. I was notoriously ham fisted when trying to cut roasts or cakes or loaves of bread, or basically trying to use a knife.

"*Non*," he said, "but it's tradition."

I gingerly poked the tower with the fork, sure that I was going to make the whole thing tumble to the floor. I speared a cream puff and managed to get it onto the plate without causing too much damage. Everyone erupted in a *ban Bourguignon*, after which I was more than happy to discreetly hand the serving utensils over to my husband.

Franck did a fantastic job dismantling the *pièce montée*. My job was to hand over the plates he gave me to the serving staff, who then distributed them to the tables.

The last two plates were for Franck and me, and we happily weaved our way back to our chairs and dug in.

I hadn't even finished savoring my first cream puff when my friend Laura-Dawn from Canada came over to me.

"Why do we have to eat horrible fruitcakes at weddings when *this* exists?" She pointed at my plate, where three remaining cream puffs festooned with lacey strings of caramel were still nestled.

"I *know!*" I said. "Right? Plum puddings. Fruitcakes. All those horrible British desserts. It's like a conspiracy or something."

"It *is* a conspiracy!" Laura-Dawn agreed. "Anyway, I'm going to get seconds."

"Wise friend," I said to Suzanne, and turned back to my plate.

Pretty much everybody, myself included, went back for seconds and thirds of the *pièce montée*. I loved how at this wedding the meal took absolute center stage. Nothing was rushed. Lucullus timed everything impeccably, allowing the perfect amount of time between courses for us to digest and chat. And then, just when we started wondering about when the next course would arrive, like magic it did. Edith Piaf warbled in the background, but I loved how nothing was rushed. That's one of the things I loved about Burgundy—there was *time* for everything.

Espressos and hard alcohols, called "*les digestifs*" in France, were distributed amongst the guests, who lingered over them.

I had noticed about an hour before dessert, the DJ had arrived and was beginning to set up his equipment at the far end of the cellar. He came over to us once he had given his lights a thorough testing, and when Franck was on his second glass of calvados.

"Are you ready for the first dance?" he asked us.

I glanced over at Franck, who downed the rest of his glass and nodded. He held out his arm to me. I stood and took it.

We had chosen the song "All of Me" by Louis Armstrong—a singer we both loved. The DJ hurried back behind his table, and the first strains of the music flowed from the massive speakers stationed on either side of the curved cellar walls.

The low, gravel voice of Louis Armstrong rumbled out next:
Yes, all of me, why not take all of me, baby?
Yes, can't you see? I'm not good without you.

Franck and I spun around the dance floor as flashes popped and people cheered. All of me…all of *us*—including the chronic lateness, the panic attacks, the ambition, the lack of practicality—we were taking *all* of each other. It just made sense because we were far better together than apart. I had never realized how appropriate the words to our chosen song were until that very moment.

Before I knew it the song was over and the high-pitched voice of France's beloved singer Claude François belting out "Cette année-la" boomed out of the speakers. Everybody stormed the dance floor, and for the next few hours, danced away to our selected mix of English and French songs—from Gloria Gaynor's "I Will Survive" to "Laura" by Johnny Hallyday. Within a few hours, I had misplaced my shoes and so had most of the other women. It was a great party, just as Franck hoped for—a visceral explosion of celebration and joy.

From time to time, I would collapse at our table for a few minutes to rehydrate with whatever I could find, whether it was water or wine. I had no idea how many hours had passed, nor did I care.

At one point, while I was passing the kitchen on my way to the washroom, my nostrils flared as they picked up the wondrous smells of onions and melting cheese and garlic. I peeked my head in and saw the kitchen staff bustling around, ladling out the French onion soup into the traditional ceramic bowls with stubby little round handles.

Franck was right. French onion soup was exactly what I felt like at…

"Can you please tell me the time?" I asked one of the serving staff.

She looked at her watch. "Almost three o'clock on the morning," she answered. "That's the traditional time for *soupe à l'oignon*."

Back in the main cellar, I told Franck that the soup was soon on its way. The news and the fragrant smell drew everyone back to their tables, and we talked and laughed and drank some more wine over spoonfuls of the shimmering onion-infused broth.

After the soup, the dancing went on for several more hours until people finally began to make their way out of the cellar. There was a flurry of "*au revoirs*," and then I collapsed onto a chair.

I was rubbing the insoles of my stocking feet when Franck returned from upstairs after helping the DJ take up the last of his equipment.

"He's on his way?" I asked.

"*Oui.*"

"He was a fantastic DJ." I held out my hand to Franck. "That was the best party I think I've ever been to. Here, help me up." We were the last ones left, just as Franck had wanted.

He hoisted me up, even though he was none too steady on his feet himself.

"One last song?" he murmured in my ear.

We had brought a CD player with the biggest speakers we could find for playing background music during the meal before the DJ arrived.

"Of course," I said. "Then after that, you're going to have to help me find my shoes."

Franck went over to the CD player and plucked a disc from the pile beside it. The sounds of Francis Cabrel's "*L'encre de tes yeux*" echoed off the vaulted walls of the now empty cellar.

"Do you remember this in Paris?" I asked.

"Why do you think I wanted this as our last dance?" Franck asked.

We had listened to this at his cousin's apartment in Paris, just before we had to leave for the airport for me to catch my plane back to Canada. We didn't know if we would ever see each other again then, and yet, here we were, married. Gratitude filled every part of my being.

We clung to each other, just as we had six years earlier, and I nestled my head in that perfect spot in the crook of his shoulder. Maybe everything in our lives wasn't perfect, but Olivier had been right. This day, in its own quirky way, had been perfect—panic attacks, rain, and all.

CHAPTER 21

Once the final chords of the song had faded away, and we had found my shoes tucked behind a decorative wine barrel in the corner of the room, we made our way up from the cellar to the land of the living, still holding hands.

I blinked in the pale, early morning light.

"We did it," Franck said, triumphant. "We celebrated all night." I could tell that this thrilled him to the depths of his Burgundian soul.

"You did an amazing job pulling all of this together." I gave him a kiss. "What time does lunch start tomorrow...or I mean, today?"

"At ten o'clock," Franck said. He wasn't wearing a watch as usual and instead squinted at the sun. "Which I would estimate would be in about four or five hours from now."

I hooked my arm in his. "Let's go to bed for a while," I said. I had grabbed my bouquet from our table in the cellar, and now clutched it with the other hand. Part of the raffia wrapped around the stems had come undone and trailed on the ground.

We made our way through the crooked cobblestoned back streets of Nuits-Saint-Georges. The hem of my wedding dress trailed after me, now distinctly dirty. I would be able to have it dry-cleaned before wearing it a second time in Canada. The streets were mostly deserted except for a few delivery trucks picking up or dropping off things at shops and wine domains. The rain and clouds had disappeared overnight, and the air was already warm.

A shrill honk made us both spin around. It was the baker, driving his *camionette* on his way to make his baguette deliveries in the surrounding villages. *"Holà! Vive la mariée!"* he exclaimed. "How was the *pièce montée?"*

"Perfection." I smiled at him. "Everyone loved it."

"Wonderful!" he looked truly gratified. *"Félicitations encore!* I must be off. There are some early risers who will be waiting for their baguettes already."

A table of several tradesmen in their faded blue work clothes having an early *café* gave me some appreciate wolf whistles. *"Vive la mariée!"* they shouted across the street. I sleepily raised my bouquet in acknowledgement of their well-wishes.

We threaded through a narrow cobblestone alley to one side of the *beffroi,* which now chimed out the half hour.

I remembered back to the day after I had first arrived in Nuits-Saint-Georges, when I came out with Madame Beaupre to do the shopping for lunch, and we stopped at each store—the grocers, the *charcuterie,* the *boulangerie,* le *crémerie*—and how strange and exotic it had all seemed to me. Part of me still found it exotic, and I thought I always would. But sometime during the previous seven years, this had become my life too, *our* life. Hopefully it would become part of our children's lives too, if we were lucky enough to have them.

Because I'd been daydreaming, I didn't realize that we had arrived at the hotel (fittingly called "la Côte d'Or") until Franck opened the heavy glass-and-brass door for me.

I thought about my corset and all the tiny buttons down the back of my wedding dress, but I wasn't feeling as energetic as I had imagined I would be feeling at this juncture. For one thing, I had pictured that we would retire to our nuptial bed when it was still actually night, not daytime. For another, my feet ached, and the Pantagruelesque wedding feast had made my body long for one thing—sleep.

I looked over to Franck as he was checking in. His normally olive complexion, come to think of it, was looking slightly paler and a tinge greener than usual.

We climbed the stairs to our suite with heavy steps.

"Enfin!" Franck said once he had unlocked the door. He collapsed backwards onto the bed with the slow, inevitable grace of a tree falling in the forest.

I did the same, but quickly became aware that no matter how I positioned myself, I was not comfortable lying down in a boned corset. Jabby things poked into my ribs and internal organs from every direction.

"I think I'm going to need your help," I said to Franck.

Franck just groaned. "Why does the ceiling spin in this hotel? Please get it to stop."

I ignored that comment, as I was experiencing the same problem. When I sat up, the whole room seemed to lurch sideways. "Whoa" I said, "I must have drank more wine than I realized."

"It wouldn't be a Burgundian wedding if that weren't the case," Franck mumbled without opening his eyes.

"I just…I need you to undo all of these buttons," I said.

Franck groaned again and sat up, clutching his head.

This scenario was diverging quite dramatically from my fantasies. I looked over my shoulder at him. "I'm glad I didn't save myself for our wedding night."

Franck snorted. "As if we could have waited that long."

He was right. He also wasn't moving to start undoing my buttons.

"You have to undo me. I can't reach back there." I flailed my hands around my back to illustrate.

"There's just…so *many* buttons. Why are there so many?" This question didn't seem so much directed at me as at the cosmos.

"It's supposed to be an erotic game to undo them slowly. You know, foreplay." I glanced back at him. His face wore an expression of bafflement and exhaustion and something else—

"You'll have to excuse me for a moment," he gasped, then ran into the bathroom and slammed the door shut behind him.

I knew what was going to happen before I heard the retching begin. It was that green shade to his skin. I should have known…

"This is super sexy!" I called out, laughing, then flopped back on the bed. The corset wouldn't let me sleep, even though every cell in my body longed to.

Franck retched again.

He emerged some time later, looking paler but decidedly less green. "So you're telling me I have to undo all those buttons before we can sleep?" He pointed at me.

"Yes," I said.

"Whoever invented dresses like this was not French. French

wedding dresses all come with zippers, I'm sure of it." Franck sat behind me on the bed and let out the most beleaguered sigh I had ever heard. I lifted my hair aside and he began to undo the tiny row of buttons.

"Did you brush your teeth after?" I asked.

"Yes."

"Because you're a romantic?" I said.

"Yes. I hope you appreciate that about me," Franck said.

"Oh, I do. Especially at the moment."

Franck had only gotten about a quarter of the way down the buttons when… "God. I feel *so* sick."

I just laughed some more. In silence except for a few sounds of frustration at the tiny, tight nature of my buttons, Franck finished unbuttoning them. He pushed the two sides of my dress apart to reveal the corset with its hundred or so little hooks and eyes underneath.

"There's more?" he exclaimed, unable to keep the horror from his voice.

"That wasn't exactly the reaction I was hoping for the first time you saw this thing."

"I'm sorry, Laura. I just don't think I can do justice to your corset tonight, or to you," he added.

"Don't you mean this morning?"

The sun was starting to shine into our bedroom in earnest, announcing a hot July day.

"Yes," Franck agreed. I turned to see him wincing at the light.

"I'm wearing this again at our Canadian reception," I said. "Remember? You can do justice to it then. I swear, for right now all I want you to do is get me out of it so that I can go to sleep."

Franck leaned forward and kissed me behind my earlobe. "You are the best wife ever."

"I know."

He got off the bed with as much dignity as he could muster. "Now I need to go and throw up again."

CHAPTER 22

I woke up completely naked with Franck shaking me. His complexion had returned to its normal shade. He also seemed annoyingly energetic.

"I let you sleep until the last moment, Laura, but you have to get up."

I glanced over to the floor beside the king-sized bed, where my wedding dress and corset were in a pile. Now it was my turn to groan. My stomach lurched. Maybe Franck had had the right idea being sick the night before.

"I think this is the worst hangover I've ever had," I said.

"You should have thrown up," Franck said, not unkindly. "I feel like a new man."

"No, no…" I carefully lay my head back on the heavenly pillow. "I think I just need to sleep a little longer."

"I can't let you do that. It's quarter after ten already. I'm sure people have started arriving. Mémé has worked so hard at making all the food."

The very mention of food made my stomach rise. I pushed Franck away with a firm hand in the middle of his chest. "Do. Not. Mention. Food."

He smiled and rubbed his stomach. "I'm hungry."

"Shut up," I said and dragged my sorry carcass to the bathroom where I stood under a scalding hot shower, which, contrary to what I had hoped, only made me feel marginally more human.

"Laura!" Franck came into the bathroom. "You have to hurry. I hung up your dress and your corset. Now that I am reborn, I have many regrets about not being in a state to appreciate them last night."

"Clothes…," I said. Even the idea of having to move my body enough to get dressed filled me with despair.

"I've laid out some clothes for you on the bed."

I walked out to find an aqua linen tunic and a pair of black, light cotton palazzo pants. Yes. They would do.

"Underwear?" I asked Franck "Bra?"

"Can't you wear that corset thing again?"

I gave him the dirtiest look imaginable.

"That would be a no," he quipped, and sped to the suitcase "Promise you'll wear it at our reception in Canada?" he said, after handing me underwear and a bra.

"I'll have to," I said, "if I'm going to wear my wedding dress again."

"Good." Franck waited for me to get dressed, his focus riveted on the corset and garters that now hung on the cupboard door.

I somehow managed to get dressed, fighting the urge to lie down and/or vomit the entire time. I scraped my hair into a makeshift twist and anchored it with my favorite silver barrette.

"There's no way I'll be able to eat," I warned Franck as we retraced our steps from a few hours earlier through the now-bustling streets of Nuits-Saint-Georges toward la Mairie.

"Mémé has been preparing this food for weeks now," Franck chided me.

"I know. I feel terrible about it, but do you remember how you felt when we got back to the hotel room?"

"I'm blocking that out of my memory."

"Well…that's exactly how I feel now."

"You should have done what I did."

Another wave of nausea crashed over me. "Let's stop talking about that. In fact, let's just stop talking."

We reached the mayor's office, where Olivier and two of Franck's cousins were smoking cigarettes above the stairs leading down to the cellars. From the amount of cars in the parking lot, I figured that most of our guests were already downstairs, ready to feast again.

"*Vive les mariés!*" Olivier shouted. He gave us a once-over and, being typically French, did not mince words. "You two are looking significantly less fresh than you did at this time yesterday." He passed

Franck a cigarette and lit it for him, then nodded at me. "Especially you, Laura. Your complexion is a most interesting shade of chartreuse."

I put my hand to my forehead and massaged it, trying to ease the pain caused by the ice-pick in my head. "I feel like death," I admitted. "*So* hungover."

"But *was* it the best day of your life?" Olivier asked me with a knowing smile.

I thought back over the day, perfect in its imperfection. "It was." I leaned beside him in the sunshine against the stone wall. "You were right," I conceded.

"I'm always right," said Olivier. It didn't sound conceited, just factual.

"What is the cure for a hangover then?" I asked, with a glimmer of hope.

"*Boire un verre, bien sûr*," Olivier said with confidence.

Hair of the dog...that was hardly original. "More wine?" I said, my voice ripe with disgust.

"I recommend something stronger. There must be a few bottles of calvados or Poire Williams left."

I gagged.

Franck stubbed out his cigarette with his heel. "We should head down," he said. "*Haut-le-coeur*, Laura!" He patted my shoulder bracingly.

I staggered down the stairs to find everybody milling around in the smaller cellar where we had held the *vin d'honneur* the day before. They were all dressed casually as Franck and I were, and looked annoyingly cheerful for a bunch of people who had only a few hours sleep, not to mention lots of wine.

When Franck and I were spotted, we were greeted with another *ban Bourguignon*, which made my head feel like it was going to explode. It was amusing to see, though, how my non-French friends had learned the song perfectly and now joined in with enthusiasm. My family weren't the only ones who had been inducted into the Burgundian way of life.

A glass of *kir* was pressed into my hand by Franck's aunt Renée. I peered at the garnet liquid, which I normally adored, and thought about Olivier's suggestion, but I still couldn't bring myself to take a sip.

I marveled that everyone except me was drinking with enthusiasm, as well as tucking away the *gougères* and mini slices of *paté en croute*, rounds of dried *saucisson sec*, and Mémé's famous *feuilletés au fromage*— little bites of puff pastry layered with Gruyère cheese. Normally I loved all those things, but not today. How was everyone else doing it?

Franck's sister, Stéphanie, came over. *"Bonjour, belle-soeur,"* she said, giving me *les bises*.

She was right, we were sisters-in-law now, although I far preferred the French expression, which translated directly into English as "beautiful sister."

"Mémé has barred all of us except Maman and Papa from the big cellar while she puts the finishing touches on her buffet. It's going to be amazing."

"It will," I agreed, somewhat half-heartedly.

"I can't wait to have some of her head cheese," Stéphanie continued. "It is one of my favorite things, and Franck's too. Do you like it?"

"Yes," I said. In fact I hated it, but I figured this answer would curtail any further discussion on the subject of head cheese more quickly than "no."

"You're not drinking your *kir*!" She chided me. "You always drink your *kir*!" She clinked her glass against mine. *"Tiens. Santé!"*

Stéphanie was a nurse. *Should I ask her about hangover cures? On second thought, probably the least amount of attention I draw to my predicament, the better.*

I took the tiniest sip possible. Luckily, just then Patrice, who was now dressed in jeans but still wore his red kerchief knotted around his neck, and Renée struck up a jaunty tune on their accordions on either side of the big sliding doors to the large cellar.

The doors opened to reveal Mémé on the other side, doing her trademark jig and clapping her hands. Everyone erupted into yet another *ban Bourguignon*.

"Les mariés! Les mariés!" She beckoned Franck and I over to her side and gave each of us a smacking *bises*, without stopping dancing for a second. With an arm slung around each of us, she propelled us toward the long table that was piled with all the food she had been preparing for months.

The food was not only plentiful beyond belief, it was beautifully presented. She had even made a massive butterfly covered with foil to present an array of slices of her homemade *terrines* and patés.

She took us to each bowl, dish, and platter on the table and gave us a personal tour of all the delicious things she had prepared. I was beyond touched. *To think of the hours of work that went into this.* It was Mémé's gift to us—and it was unforgettable. Still, I kept having to swallow hard as she pointed out the jellied pigs' feet and the *fromage de tête*, which she knew I hated. She found this to be a glorious joke and set off into gales of laughter.

We both kissed her, and she took her leave of us, continuing to dance around the room to Renée and Patrice's accordions as she accepted accolades from her many admirers in the crowd.

Everybody, I observed with astonishment, couldn't wait to dig in. I wanted so badly to feel hungry, or at least not feel such a strong aversion to any food or drink, but wishing was not working.

I sat down at the table, sipping only at a large glass of water, my glass of *kir* and a glass of wine ignored.

Olivier came over to check on me just as Mémé noticed I didn't, unlike most people, have a plate piled high with buffet items in front of me. They converged on me at the same time.

"Laura! You have nothing to eat yet!" she pulled me up with an iron grip to my upper arm. Olivier observed me under drawn brows.

"I was just chatting with everyone," I said. "Don't worry. There's no rush."

"But there is!" she squeezed my arm for emphasis. "The food might run out." I surveyed the gargantuan spread and knew that the kitchen was also full of replacement dishes to fill any holes as people ate. The Burgundian fear of running out of food was truly pathological, especially in Franck's family.

"Come! Come!" She led me to the buffet and thrust a plate in my hand. Luckily, before she could actually fill up my plate for me, Franck's aunt Jacqueline rushed in to let Mémé know that her culinary expertise was required immediately in the kitchen. Something about the nut bread to be served with the cheese.

As I had no appetite, I filled up my plate without any true intention of eating anything on it, but rather to blend in with the crowd and, more importantly, to not hurt Mémé's feelings.

When I got back to the table, I was surprised to see Olivier hovering near my chair, waiting for me with a *trou Normand* in his hand like the ones we had the night before.

"I snuck in the kitchen and made this especially for you, but you have to eat it fast," he said.

"Wha—?"

"I said it was for Michel." That was one of Franck's many cousins, who had been distinctly worse for wear last night but who now looked like he was raring to go again—damn his eyes. "You will feel the better for it, I promise. Come with me." He beckoned me to the far end of the cellar where hidden behind a funny angle in the curved wall was a stone staircase that I hadn't noticed before.

"This is all very mysterious," I said as I followed him up the dark stairs. He opened a metal trap door at the top, and we found ourselves in the manicured French gardens at the back of la Mairie.

He whipped a spoon out of his back pocket and then sat down on the stone ledge to the staircase. I sat down beside him and he passed me the small glass goblet and the spoon.

I stared down at the white sorbet swimming in alcohol. "Poire Williams?" I asked.

"Calvados," he said.

"I don't know if I will be able to keep this down, Olivier," I confided.

He clicked his tongue disparagingly. "You have to trust me. Was I right about yesterday?"

"Yes," I admitted.

"I'm right about this too," he said, then reached over and lifted my hand so the goblet was closer to my mouth. "Eat up."

I sighed and took a spoonful, then swallowed. It was technically more a matter of slurping than eating. The sunshine was already scorching and the sorbet had mostly melted, leaving a highly alcoholic slushy for me to slurp back.

I coughed. "Rather heavy-handed with the calvados, *n'est-ce pas?*"

"I had to be," Olivier said, unrepentant. "That's the medicinal component."

After abandoning my spoon on the step beside me, I took a deep breath, tipped back the glass, and let the slushy slide into my mouth in almost one go. I let out a strange noise, a cross between a growl and a roar. "In the name of God, that was strong." I put the glass beside the spoon.

Olivier extracted a package of cigarette papers and a sachet of loose tobacco from his jean's pocket and began to patiently roll up a cigarette.

"Now we just need to wait for about five minutes."

Surprisingly, I didn't feel like the *trou Normand* was going to make a return trip from my stomach. My gut actually felt slightly more settled, I realized with something akin to disbelief.

I tilted my face up to the sun and remained like that, soaking it in for a few minutes, until Olivier spoke again. "How are you doing now?"

I took a silent inventory of my stomach and actually felt a little gurgle of, not nausea, but hunger. My eyelids flew open. "*Mon Dieu. I do* feel better. I think it may have worked."

"Told you," he said, lining up the four rolled cigarettes he had made while waiting in his shirt pocket like a row of soldiers. "Now let's get you back down to the cellar before la Mémé notices."

"Thank you, Olivier," I said, leaning over and giving him *les bises.*

He shrugged. "What are friends for?"

Olivier's cure was magical indeed. It not only enabled me to enjoy a bit of almost everything on Mémé's buffet (with the notable exception of the head cheese), but also to partake in more of Franck's uncle's wine, yet another incredible cheese platter, and, best of all, the selection of twelve different cakes, which Mémé paraded into the cellar with great fanfare to much accordion music and dancing.

Before I knew it, we were all pitching in with the cleanup. My family from London (my great-aunt Marigold and my uncle Arthur, along with my cousin Julia) dried dishes as Jacqueline and Jean washed them. They all worked like Trojans, having a merry old time and dancing and singing, despite the fact that they did not share a common language.

Mémé and the bossy Geneviève had plucked flowers from the

various bouquets staggered around the room and were nimbly fashioning them into "bridal bouquets" to hand out to all the females. This evolved into a great show of everyone pretending to be a bride and walking down a makeshift aisle in the hallway between the cellars and the kitchens with the most unlikely of partners. The ultimate was my great-uncle Arthur and Jean who paraded down the pretend aisle to general cheers and much laughter, with Jean carrying the bridal bouquet and tall, gawky Arthur wearing a quickly fashioned wreath of vineyard leaves.

By the time we emerged from the cellars, it was dark again and the stars were bright in the inky sky.

The wedding was well and truly over. The next morning, we would be leaving with my parents and Canadian family to spend a week in Provence for a rather strange type of honeymoon, if you could call it that.

I silently thanked the stars for aligning for Franck and me, and for bringing us here to this place and this point in time, together.

CHAPTER 23

Franck and I were in the attic of his house in Villers-la-Faye, sprawled on the couch watching TV. My parents had just left for Canada that morning, and we were due to fly out the next morning with Franck's family, Jean, and Jacqueline to continue our wedding celebrations in Canada. We were watching a rerun of the classic movie *La Grande Vadrouille*, which is set during the Second World War and was shot mostly in and around Beaune.

Life as a married couple was still fresh and, just as they did when I traveled to a different country for the first time, the small things struck me. *Le facteur* had brought my first piece of mail addressed to "Mme Laura Germain" that morning. It was from the French tax department, but still… I had held the envelope in my hands and stared at the words for several minutes. Mme Germain. That wasn't just Franck's mother now. It was me too. Franck had taken to frequently calling me *"ma femme."* My wife. And there was something new when we woke up in the morning together. The knowledge that no matter what that day would bring, or the ones after that, we had once and for all time thrown in our lots with one another.

It wasn't going to be easy getting through the next year at Oxford, not to mention my final exams, but we would have the memories of our crazy Burgundian wedding.

I thought back to Dr. Pradhan in Nepal saying to me, "Life is tragedy and life is joy and life is mostly everything messy in between." Maybe we all were like that. Maybe *marriage* was like that.

I was still contemplating this novel concept when the phone rang. I paused our movie.

"*Allô?*" Franck answered. "Yes. This is Monsieur Franck Germain…" The conversation didn't sound too earth shattering. Franck kept nodding and making sounds while I pressed play on the remote control and began watching the movie again. I was vaguely aware of his exclamations, and then as he hung up, laughter.

"What?" I rolled over on the couch.

"You're not going to believe it," he said.

"Try me."

"That was the mayor's office."

"Really? What did they want?"

"They need us to come down there and sign some forms before we leave."

"What forms?"

"Well…" Franck took the remote control from my hands and turned off the film again. I let out a sound of protest. "No," he said, "you're going to want to hear this."

"Hear what?"

"That was the secretary at la Mairie. Turns out the substitute *maire*— as dapper as he might have been—didn't do his paperwork properly."

"So?"

"So, we're not actually married after all."

I just stared at him for a few seconds. Franck wasn't my husband, after all that? "You're kidding me," I said.

"I'm not. I swear."

"So, we're not officially married until we go down and sign those forms? Even after our perfectly imperfect wedding?"

"Nope."

"So, what we did last night—"

"Sinful." Franck clicked his tongue in mock censure. "*Très* sinful."

Our eyes met, and we both laughed until we were bent over holding our stomachs and gasping for air. When we calmed down a bit, he took my hand in his.

"So, Laura." Franck seemed to be having a difficult time mustering up a grave look. "Do you want to come with me to la Mairie right now and get married…again?"

"I do."

We strolled through the blue July day to get married a third time—just the two of us.

La Fin

Books by Laura Bradbury

Grape Series

(suggested reading order)

My Grape Year

My Grape Wedding

My Grape Escape

My Grape Village

Other Writings:

Philosophy of Preschoolers

MERCI

I suppose I must thank the writing muses because even now it's finished, it is a complete mystery to me how I actually managed to write and publish *My Grape Wedding*. This year has been one of the hardest in my life. My auto-immune bile duct and liver disease (PSC) has not only made me extremely ill, but also jettisoned me into an existence where I spend most of my time coordinating or undergoing medical testing and appointments. This culminated in the news ten days ago that I have (finally!) been accepted as a transplant candidate at the University of Alberta Hospital's liver transplant center in Edmonton.

A life-saving liver transplant brings along with it great risks but as the alternative at this point is certain death, it is a risk I am not just willing, but eager, to take.

My experiences of the past year, and surely the year ahead of me, could fill several books all on their own. If I get through this storm, those are books I will write. I know myself though - I am only able to write about experiences once they are behind me.

In the meantime, here are three of the many lessons I have learned so far:

1. Never put off living, no matter what your age – For God sakes, take that dream trip, smile at that stranger, spend time chatting with your kids, eat that delicious cheese, paint that picture, write that book, build that yurt in your backyard...whatever you dream of try and find a way to do it. Being alive is a terminal condition, so don't delude yourself into thinking you have unlimited time. None of us do, not even the macrobiotic raw-food vegans.

2. Fear is life's greatest illusion – I always viewed fear as a solid, tangible thing, like a wall that stood between me and a full life. I was scared of so many things; elevators, walking alone after dark, earthquakes, being a failed writer, traveling on airplanes...yet all these fears and many more simply evaporated

the day I was diagnosed with PSC. Even though they felt so threatening, my fears ended up being less substantial than the water droplets that make up a cloud. These days I am pretty much only scared by the prospect of dying and leaving my girls without their mother, but I know now that even this fear has no substance. Fear is life's biggest trickster. Walk straight through it just as you would a foggy morning. Do not let it stop you from doing anything.

3. There is no "us" and "them" – I need a person to voluntarily donate part of their liver to save my life. Incredible people *have* stepped forward and are now undergoing testing to see if they are, indeed, a match for me. In this age of political divisiveness, xenophobia, and poorly concealed racism I think more than ever we need to remember that we are all interconnected. If everything goes well, I will be walking around for the rest of my life with a part of someone else inside of me, keeping me alive. How could I ever believe that I am separate from any other human being after such a gesture? How could I ever look at someone else as competition or a threat? The answer is I cannot. That certainty is, perhaps, the greatest gift of all. We all sleep under the same sky.

So thank you to those extraordinary people who have applied to be potential liver donors for me. You have shown me a transcendent aspect of humanity that has forever changed me and lights a clear path forward for however many days I have left on this earth.

Thank you to my (large) medical team, from my GI and hepatologists to my transplant coordinators to my pharmacists and the lovely women at Lifelabs that make the endless bloodwork a fun social event. A special shout-out to Alicia who always goes the extra mile (make that extra 100 miles) for me. I couldn't have qualified for transplant without her efficient assistance.

A massive *merci* to all my wonderful readers who have embraced my memoirs, transformed them into bestsellers, and are an unflagging source of encouragement on my good and bad writing days. I apologize here for not getting back to readers who have sent me such kind and supportive emails over the past six months. Qualifying for transplant is a full-time job I've discovered, but please know I read every message and they never fail to give me a boost during the difficult times. I promise I will be a better correspondent when I get this sick liver replaced!

I set out to write My Grape Wedding as a novella (20-40,000 words) but over the months it morphed into 54,000 words. This means it is too long for a novella, but still on the short side for a novel. This is the first time I have ever written a book of this size before, but I have discovered that books are a bit like babies – they come out the way they come out and I have little say in the matter. Next up will be My Grape Paris which *will* be a full-sized book encompassing a calendar year. I'm almost half way through the rough draft and am already eager to get it into your hands.

Thank you Eileen Cook for an insightful content edit, *comme d'habitude* and congratulations on her enormous writing success this year. Do yourself a favor and pick up a copy of her latest book, the riveting "With Malice".

A herd of a million bisons for my beloved friend Pamela Patchet for just being an amazing human being, as well as a brilliant beta reader and tagline / blurb writer. She is the fairy godmother of all of my 'Grape' books. I can't wait to get a new liver and go mudlarking with her on the Thames.

Mary-Ellen Reid did an amazing copy-edit as usual. My Grape Wedding would not be nearly as polished without her genius with detail. Paul always does an amazing job of formatting and saves me from throwing my computer out the window. Rebecca Sky has once again created a stunning cover and I have Krystal Kenney to thank for taking the cover photo again in Paris and perfectly converting the image stuck in my mind into reality.

Thank you to my family and all my friends in Victoria, France, and elsewhere around the globe, as well as my writing tribe from the Surrey International Writers' Conference (www.siwc.ca). All those good thoughts, vibes, and prayers truly do make a huge difference.

As always, I owe a huge debt of gratitude to the PSC community at PSC Partners Seeking a Cure. I keep the memory of Sandi Pearlman and Phillip Burke close to my heart and I try to follow their example of using my PSC as a catalyst for good in the world. To that end, 10% of all after-tax royalties of everything I write are donated to PSC Partners

Seeking a Cure for much-needed research.

http://www.pscpartners.org/ .

I urge everyone to sign up to be an organ donor and to support an opt-out system in their country. The current organ donation system in Canada and the United States is broken. People die every day waiting for potentially life-saving organ transplants. In Canada you can sign this petition:

https://www.gopetition.com/petitions/save-lives-through-presumed-organ-donation.html .

Also, all PSCers out there need to sign up for our patient registry and help speed up much-needed research to find a cure for this currently incurable disease. Here is the link:

https://pscpartners.patientcrossroads.org/ .

Thank you to Franck who has been an absolute rock during the "in sickness" portion of our "in sickness and in health" wedding vows. I would marry him again in a heartbeat.

Last of all, thank you to Charlotte, Camille, and Clémentine for being such constant sources of inspiration. At a pre-transplant assessment meeting a social worker suggested I prepare for my death by writing letters to each of my daughters in case I don't make it to or through transplant surgery. I thought about this for a second and then answered, "Actually, I already *have* written to my girls. It's just that I wrote books instead of letters and published them...".

That's ultimately what the 'Grape' series is about at its heart – book-sized love letters to my girls that tell the tale of where they came from and things I have learned along the way.

I still have many more stories to tell, so wish me *bonne chance*!